Music

Curriculum Writing 101

Assistance with Standards-based Music Curriculum and Assessment Writing

Music
Curriculum Writing 101

Assistance with Standards-based Music Curriculum and Assessment Writing

For Band, Choir, Orchestra, and General Music

Denese Odegaard

GIA Publications, Inc.
Chicago

Music Curriculum Writing 101
Denese Odegaard

G-7341
ISBN: 978-1-57999-724-3

Copyright © 2009 GIA Publications, Inc.
7404 S Mason Ave
Chicago IL 60638

www.giamusic.com

Contents

Chapter 3   **Suggested Activities for Each National Standard**

Preface

This book will change the way you think about what and how you teach, align your curriculum to the ever-changing world of education, and guide you through the processes of writing a standards-based curriculum and assessments *for* student learning.

WHO IS THIS BOOK FOR?

This book is for future or present music instructors desiring to develop a standards-based, comprehensive curriculum and assessments—one in which students will be engaged learners.

HELP WITH THREE SIMPLE STEPS: S. O. S.

This book will help with the following three processes in developing a standards-based curriculum and assessments:

Sequence   curriculum throughout the year so that music unfolds for the student. This replaces teaching "from cover to cover," which may not meet the needs of the curriculum.

Organize   curriculum and documentation of student progress. Start the year with a plan and there will be more teacher free time and fewer discipline problems during the year.

Standards   are here to stay and they change the breadth of musical knowledge students acquire during their educational journey, producing better musicians over time. Pairing with a standards-based curriculum is assessment. *Curriculum Writing 101* will cover how to write, execute, document, distribute, and store student assessments.

WHY DO YOU NEED A STANDARDS-BASED CURRICULUM?

So many times teachers become comfortable in their own style of teaching and continue to teach students in the way they have found successful or the way in which they were taught. Sometimes there is no direction or purpose in what they teach or a balanced curriculum is not offered. There may be a better way to reach students so that they recognize their full potential.

In our ever-changing world, curricula should be ever-changing as well. Final curriculum documents should be a works in progress, updating constantly to the current trends in education.

MENC (Music Educators National Conference) created National Music Standards in the early 1990s and those standards are here to stay. They have proven to be a better way for students to learn. Not only did music educators develop standards, but every subject has standards to be met. This creates a consistent learning environment across a school district so that when students transfer to other schools, they are able to continue with their music education in a similar fashion as at the last school they attended. If standards have proven effective in every other subject area, why should music be any different?

By having a standards-based curriculum in place, teachers demonstrate to administrators that they are current with education ideals and that the music program is as educationally sound as other subjects. When or if budget cuts occur, the music program is secured through the curriculum.

HOW DO YOU MAKE TIME FOR ALL OF THIS?

Curriculum Writing 101 will answer that question. I am not going to say it is easy. On some days you will feel like you are juggling several things in the classroom, and you may occasionally use your personal time, but the end product is worth the extra time and effort.

Simple "chunking" of standards or creating lesson plans using more than one standard in an activity makes teaching efficient. Quick assessment and documentation are also addressed. By organizing the curriculum, lesson plans, and documentation, students learn more in a shorter period of time, reaching higher goals and becoming active participants in their own education.

WHAT IS IN IT FOR YOU?

Putting in the extra time to develop a well-thought-out curriculum and assessments will give you direction in your teaching, reduce discipline problems, engage students, and prove the longevity of your program to your administration.

If you are absent from school for a period of time, your sub will know exactly what to cover next without you worrying if students' needs are being met.

Working together with other music staff members in creating a curriculum is a great learning experience. All teachers involved in curriculum writing bring new ideas and teaching approaches to the table. The discussions enrich you as a teacher and create a cohesive staff.

Students want to succeed and improve, and parents and students want to be involved in a superb program.

Acknowledgments

First I would like to thank my family, Ron, Erin and Amy, who have allowed me to take the time to develop this material which I have used not only in the classroom, but for presentations at state and national conventions which takes me away from home often.

Second, a number of music educators need to be thanked. These valuable teachers are experts and have helped draft some of the assessments and curriculum found in this book:

- The Fargo Public Schools Music Teachers, Fargo, North Dakota
- Joan Eckroth-Riley, Bismarck Public Schools, Bismarck, North Dakota
- Nancy Ditmer, Professor of Music at The College of Wooster, Wooster, Ohio
- William Guegold, The University of Akron College, Director of the School of Music, Akron, Ohio
- Eric Doolittle, Worthington City Schools, Worthington, Ohio
- Jay Wardeska, Brunswick City Schools, Brunswick, Ohio
- Jean Smith, Marion Local Schools, Maria Stein, Ohio

Next are the hundreds of students I have taught over the past twenty-five years. They have allowed me to experiment with new ideas and have provided valuable feedback.

Thank you to GIA Publications, which has given me a great opportunity to share this information with many music instructors. I am thrilled to help others make their job more engaging, efficient, successful, and secure.

How to Use This Book

Curriculum Writing 101 examines how to write a standards-based curriculum using the following steps:

1. Obtain a copy of the MENC national standards document.
2. Check with your state to see how they have adapted the document.
3. Write your own district curriculum in the areas of band, choir, orchestra, and general music, along with the consideration of jazz band, special music learners, music composition, or other subjects that are offered in your district.
4. Write your curriculum by grade level for each of the genres listed in step three.
5. Include in the document:
    Standards.
    Benchmarks.
    Learning targets or specific knowledge students need to know at each grade level.
    Performance tasks or activities that may be used to teach the learning targets.
6. From the list of specific knowledge required for each level in the curriculum document, create a knowledge base document for each grade level so that students and teachers know what is expected of them for the school year.
7. Identify Power Standards. Teach all of the standards and benchmarks, but select a list of critical benchmarks to cover for each grade level.
8. From the curriculum, decide what benchmarks or benchmark items you need to assess and create a list to be used as a progress report or portfolio page.
9. Assessments from chapter 7 can be used or adapted for your needs when assessing students. Always give students a copy of the assessment prior to assessing so they know the expectations. Remember, students are able to assess themselves and others.
10. Keep assessments simple so that they may be executed quickly without interrupting class time. Create quick documentation forms so that scores may be entered with ease.
11. Reporting assessments to parents at conference, supervisors, and students is important, not only to communicate the value of your course, but to let students know what they are doing well and how they can improve.

IMPORTANT TO REMEMBER

If you create curriculum documents for each genre by grade level and assess students, your program is strengthened and is less volatile in the event of reductions or cuts. Music *is* a core subject to be treated equal to all other subjects by teachers and administrators alike.

SUGGESTIONS FOR WRITING A CURRICULUM

In many school districts, a few people get together during the summer and write a curriculum. I suggest that you take professional development days and involve the entire music staff. School districts now offer curriculum writing compensation or release time as well. It is well worth the time to have the input from every teacher, and the time you share brings unity to the staff. The invaluable discussions that result are vital to all teachers understanding the curriculum decisions being made. Granted, there will be a minority who don't want to get involved, but they will eventually change their minds as they see how they can learn new things from their peers.

During curriculum writing, it is important that an overview of the writing project is presented to the whole music staff. Each area or genre needs to align to the others using the same writing guidelines.

Establish meeting norms prior to your work sessions so that staff remains professional and respectful of others' opinions. This also maximizes your use of time if members are kept on track with goals set. Agreeing to disagree at times is a necessity.

It is best to have each genre split into grade-level groups to write specifically for each particular level. It may become evident that some teachers don't push their students enough while others teach more advanced concepts than they should for a particular level. This becomes a checks-and-balances opportunity.

Once grade levels are completed, all teachers of a particular genre should return to meet together to review sequencing of the curriculum from grade to grade. Examining curriculum from grade to grade fills gaps in instruction, and eliminates duplications.

From the completed curriculum, teachers in a particular genre should meet with teachers of other grade levels to determine what to assess. A completed list allows assessments to be written. Assessments are written prior to making decisions on what materials or activities will be used to teach particular concepts. This follows the model of *Understanding by Design* by Grant Wiggins and Jay McTighe. Decide what you want students to know, write the assessment, and then decide what and how you will teach the material. See chapter 7 on writing assessments.

FURTHER CONSIDERATIONS

Once the curriculum is in place, assessments can be written. Take time to share ideas on assessments and write a trial rubric. Record student performances and use rubrics you have written to practice assessing as a group of teachers. It is beneficial to hear opinions of others and come to a consensus on how to assess. You need to appropriately define exemplary, progressing, and beginning stages for each grade level.

Since what you teach may be different from previous instruction, you may need resources. As a district staff, determine what will enhance your instruction and requisition those resources. Some school districts have a supplementary resource list through which all teachers are able to receive equal resources so that all students receive the same instruction. Some technology equipment may need to be shared within a department. Make sure you have a check-out chart so that you have equipment when needed.

WORKING TOGETHER

Teach each other.

Evaluate your curriculum often.

Align all genres to state standards.

Make time to change.

Work together—share expertise and ideas.

Organize and sequence your teaching materials to address the standards.

Revise, review, and revise some more.

Keep communication with your colleagues open. You are all experts.

Chapter 1

Overview of the National and State Music Standards Documents

OVERVIEW OF THE MENC NATIONAL MUSIC STANDARDS

MENC (Music Educators National Conference) wrote the National Music Standards in the early 1990s. At the time of this writing, these standards have been around close to twenty years. This proves standards are not a disappearing trend.

The MENC document evolved through many years, just as it will take several years to write, re-write, and refine your own curriculum documents. Refinement is not the end of the road for your document; it is a work in progress that will change frequently as educational research and trends change.

The nine national music standards are:

Standard 1: SINGING
Standard 2: INSTRUMENTAL PERFORMANCE
Standard 3: IMPROVISATION
Standard 4: COMPOSITION
Standard 5: READING MUSIC
Standard 6: LISTENING
Standard 7: EVALUATING MUSIC
Standard 8: MUSIC AND OTHER DISCIPLINES
Standard 9: MUSIC, HISTORY, AND CULTURE

The MENC document contains standards and benchmarks for dance, music, theater, and visual arts. The standards and benchmarks (achievement standards) list what is to be accomplished by the end of Grades 4, 8, and 12.

When writing your own curriculum, keep in mind to write for each separate grade level. What is written for each grade needs to align within the guidelines of each section of the document: Grades K–4, 5–8, and 9–12.

OBTAINING THE NATIONAL MENC STANDARDS DOCUMENT

To purchase the national MENC music standards document, call the MENC office at 1–800–828–0229 or go to the website http://menc.org. The publication is called *National Standards for Arts Education: What Every Young American Should Know and Be Able to Do in the Arts* (ISBN 1–56545–036–1 #1605).

Two other publications that may be helpful are *Performance Standards for Music: Strategies and Benchmarks for Assessing Progress Towards the National Standards, Grades Pre-K–12* (ISBN 1–56545–099–X #1633) and *Performing with Understanding: The Challenge of the National Standards for Music Education* (ISBN 1–56545–118–X. #1672).

CONTENT STANDARDS AND BENCHMARKS

Content Standard

For each standard, there is a general statement that describes what students should know and be able to do.

Benchmarks

Benchmarks are set points for grades 4, 8, and 12 that specifically describe knowledge and skills. These are called achievement standards in the original document and are listed under the content standard.

For example:

Standard 1: SINGING. *Students sing, alone and with others, a varied repertoire of music.* This is the standard.

4.1.1. *Sing independently on pitch and in rhythm.* This is the benchmark.

The first number of the three before the benchmark is the grade level; the second is the standard number, and the third is the benchmark number. So 4.1.1 indicates Grade 4, Standard 1, and Benchmark 1.

PERFORMANCE STANDARDS

In 1996, MENC published *Performance Standards for Music,* which provides strategies and benchmarks for assessing progress toward the national standards. Each level has a statement that describes the degrees of proficiency that are expected of students for each standard. The three levels are:

Basic	The beginning stages of mastery and progression toward proficiency.
Proficient	Students master what is expected at the grade levels stated (grades 4, 8, and 12).
Advanced	This level is significantly above the proficient level, showing the exceptional abilities of some students through ease of concept mastery, expression, or creativity.

Since the writing of this MENC publication, a four-level rubric has become the norm:

Level 4	Exceptional ease or creativity (Advanced).
Level 3	What is expected at grade level: mastery of skill or concept (Proficient).
Level 2	Understanding and working toward mastery of a skill or concept (Partially Proficient).
Level 1	Beginning stages of working toward learning a skill or concept (Novice).

Levels 1 and 2 should never give the student a feeling of failure. Every student is at a different level in understanding and executing concepts, and some simply remain at the beginning stages longer than others. Always mention to the student growth that is observed, how they are heading toward the goal, or if they have exceeded the goal. Refer to chapter 7 for more detail on assessments.

VIEWING STATE STANDARDS DOCUMENTS

Many states have taken the national standards document and adapted it to a format that makes sense to their music instructors. Search the web for state standards documents to see different versions and adaptations of the national standards.

Some states have opted to keep the same format as the national standards, while some have grouped them into categories. Sadly, some states may not have fine arts standards at all.

Chapter 2

Aligning District Standards to the National or State Standards

DOCUMENT FORMAT

The organization of a district standards document is crucial to the sequence of what is taught and when. If all teachers in each specific genre of band, orchestra, choir, and general music work together in creating a curriculum document, then they have the opportunity to give input and will take ownership of the document. Other courses that should have a curriculum may include jazz band, special learners adaptive music, jazz choir, chamber orchestra, or musical theater.

Many times two or three teachers write the curriculum for all of the teachers, some of whom may not agree with what is written. When all teachers are involved in the process, the discussions they have during curriculum writing help them understand what is important to teach at each grade level. New teachers entering the school system will have a clear picture of what they should teach as well.

The first step is to follow the national standards format, listing each standard and benchmark individually using the exact wording. This is a clear and clean-cut way to ensure that all nine standards are included in your document.

A typical format is:

Standard	
Benchmark	
Specific Knowledge	Labeling the exact knowledge a student should demonstrate at a particular grade level. Note that these are labeled Specific Knowledge in the MENC document, but could also be called Learning Targets.
Performance Tasks	Activities that can be used to teach and practice the knowledge to be acquired at each grade level.

Figure 1 gives an example of grade 5 beginning strings:

Figure 1.
Sample District Standards Document for Grade 5 Beginning Strings

Standard	SINGING
	Students sing alone and with others, a varied repertoire of music.
Benchmark	
1.8.1.5	Sing accurately and with good breath control throughout their singing ranges, alone and in small and large groups.
Specific Knowledge	Demonstrate the ability to match pitches of a tuning note or short phrase.
Performance Tasks	1. Students vocally echo a 2–5 beat melody demonstrated by the teacher. 2. Students individually sing question and answer statements. 3. Students individually sing phrases before playing.

1.8.1.5 indicates the first standard, grades 4–8 (on the national document), the first benchmark, and grade 5 for your district.

SPECIFIC KNOWLEDGE

In writing statements of the specific knowledge a student must demonstrate, it is best to use higher-level thinking, such as verbs found in *Bloom's Taxonomy:*

Knowledge

arrange	label	name	relate	reproduce
define	list	order	recall	state
duplicate	memorize	recognize	repeat	

Examples:　1. Define terms
　　　　　　2. Label rhythms and notes
　　　　　　3. Repeat musical demonstrations of articulations

Comprehension

classify	explain	indicate	report	select
describe	express	locate	restate	translate
discuss	identify	recognize	review	

Examples: 1. Describe elements of music

                2. Recognize symbols and their meanings

                3. Translate Italian musical terms into English

Application

apply   dramatize   interpret   schedule   use

choose   employ   operate   sketch   write

demonstrate   illustrate   practice   solve

Examples: 1. Apply musical knowledge to an unknown musical selection

                2. Demonstrate an articulation

                3. Practice new material

                4. Write an evaluation of a performance

Analysis

analyze   categorize   criticize   distinguish   question

appraise   compare   differentiate   examine   test

calculate   contrast   discriminate   experiment

Examples: 1. Analyze the form of a musical selection

                2. Experiment with notes and rhythms to write a musical composition

                3. Compare and contrast different recordings or performances of a piece

Synthesis

arrange   compose   design   manage   prepare write

assemble   construct   develop   organize   propose

collect   create   formulate   plan   set up

Examples: 1. Arrange a simple melody

                2. Compose a piece of music

                3. Prepare a piece of music for performance

Evaluation

appraise   attach   defend   predict   select   evaluate

argue   choose   estimate   rate   support

assess   compare   judge   core   value

Examples: 1. Assess the quality of a performance by others or self

                2. Self-evaluate or predict the steps to practicing a new piece

It is necessary to know information when it comes to reading music, but mainstream education is capturing a broader base of thinking, such as analyzing, synthesis, and evaluation. Standards6–9 tend to use these higher-level thinking skills.

PERFORMANCE TASKS

This section lists specific activities that support the standard, benchmark, and specific knowledge categories. With other staff members, brainstorm strategies for introducing and practicing concepts, keeping in mind how to assess these areas. This allows teachers to learn from and understand each other better, with the end result being a more cohesive curriculum and increased participation by all teachers.

When creating a curriculum by grade level, keep in mind that activities can start out simply and then increase in complexity through the years of music study.

EXAMPLES OF SPECIFIC KNOWLEDGE AND PERFORMANCE TASKS

STANDARD 1: SINGING. GRADE 6 CHOIR

1.8.1.6   ***Sing accurately and with good breath control throughout their singing ranges, alone, and in small and large groups***

Specific Knowledge

Produce pure vowels and clear consonants with good tone quality.

Performance Tasks

1. Sing a familiar warm-up exercise, exhibiting pure, open vowels.
2. Sing a familiar melody or exercise, exhibiting clear, clean consonants with good tone quality.

Specific Knowledge

Develop singing alignment with:

feet shoulder-distance apart

soft knees

ribcage lifted

hands at sides

shoulders back and relaxed

head centered over body with chin parallel to the floor

a straight back

Performance Tasks
1. Develop accurate singing alignment through warm-ups.
2. Exhibit accurate singing alignment throughout rehearsal when singing.

Specific Knowledge
Develop good breathing technique, which exhibits free air passage and diaphragmatic support.

Performance Tasks
Demonstrate good breathing technique through specially designed exercises

Specific Knowledge
Demonstrate accurate intonation and rhythm.

Performance Tasks
1. Demonstrate pitch accuracy by singing a rehearsed warm-up or melody.
2. Sing familiar intervals given in unfamiliar flashcards, exercises, or musical excerpts.
3. Accurately clap specific rhythm patterns in familiar and unfamiliar flashcards, exercises, or musical excerpts.

1.8.2.6   *Sing with expression and technical accuracy a repertoire of vocal literature*
Specific Knowledge
Perform with:
     accurate interval relationships
     proper phrasing
     accurate pitch and rhythm
     interpretation and understanding of text, along with a variation of dynamics

Performance Tasks
Demonstrate individually and as a group the emotional and musical technical demands of various selections (memorized and non-memorized).

1.8.3.6   *Sing music representing diverse genres and cultures*
Specific Knowledge
Demonstrate individually and as a group:
     appropriate singing style for various styles of music in regard to rhythmic
        interpretations
     melodic treatment
     pronunciation and enunciation
     other specific elements

Performance Tasks

Demonstrate appropriate vocal style while singing:

spirituals	pop
patriotic	multicultural music
folk song	traditional choral literature from the Renaissance, Baroque, and Classical periods

1.8.4.6   ***Sing music written in two and three parts***

Specific Knowledge

Perform in a group and/or independently:

ostinato	partner songs
descant	rounds
counterparts	

Performance Tasks

Sing independent parts during:

rounds

partner songs

choral music with multiple staves

STANDARD 2: INSTRUMENTAL PERFORMANCE. GRADE 9 ORCHESTRA

Note: E designates grades 9–12 in the MENC document or "Exit."

2.E.1.9   ***Perform with expression and technical accuracy***

Specific Knowledge

Demonstrate in a variety of keys and styles:

listening	phrasing	rhythms
rubato	interpretation	
dynamics	various meters	

Performance Tasks

1. Apply knowledge of expression, tone quality, and technical accuracy through performance of literature, alone and in groups. Describe and support an interpretation of this literature.
2. Perform one-to-two-octave scales and literature in the major and minor keys up to three flats or sharps.

Specific Knowledge
Understand and demonstrate:

vibrato	playing in positions	intonation
articulation	tone	
proper posture	style	

Performance Tasks
Develop and demonstrate using current repertoire:

> proper position
> posture
> playing techniques

> Violinists play in positions I–V.
> Violists play in positions I–V.
> Cellists play in positions I–IV.
> Bassists play in positions I–IV.

2.E.2.9   ***Perform in an ensemble***

Specific Knowledge
Practice ensemble skills:

> balance
> intonation
> rhythmic unity
> tone

Performance Tasks
Learn and practice the elements of music and independence of line to perform parts in an ensemble experience.

2.E.3.9   ***Perform in small ensembles with one on a part***

Specific Knowledge
Demonstrate:

> musical independence
> listening skills
> blending
> cooperation

Performance Tasks
Perform in a small ensemble of two-to-twelve people with one-to-two per part. The ensemble plays without a conductor and unaccompanied. The literature is comparable to grade 3 literature.

STANDARD 3: IMPROVISATION. GRADE 7 (ALL GENRES)

3.8.1.7   ***Improvise simple harmonic accompaniments***
Specific Knowledge
Improvise an accompaniment based on the root of the tonic, subdominant, and dominant chords while another student, group, or teacher plays a melody.

Performance Tasks
Determine where chord changes occur while improvising an accompaniment to a simple melody and make proper chord changes using a rhythmic pattern of choice.

3.8.2.7   ***Improvise melodic embellishments and simple rhythmic and melodic variations***
Specific Knowledge
Improvise melodic embellishments and simple rhythmic and melodic variations on given pentatonic melodies and melodies in major keys.

Performance Tasks
Improvise a melodic variation using neighboring or chordal tones on a given or original melody.

3.8.3.7   ***Improvise short melodies, unaccompanied and over given rhythmic accompaniments***
Specific Knowledge
Understand how to mix given notes and rhythms in a steady tempo, with or without accompaniment, which may include:

    quarter notes and rests
    eighth notes and rests
    sixteenth notes
    dotted-eighth notes
    eighth-note triplets
    dotted-quarter notes and rests
    half notes and rests
    whole notes and rests
    dotted half notes
    syncopated rhythms using eighth-quarter-eighth or sixteenth-eighth-sixteenth
        combinations
    tied notes
    combinations of the above-mentioned note values in these meters:

2/4	2/2
3/4	3/8
4/4	6/8

Performance Tasks

Improvise a melody using a given set of notes and rhythms.

STANDARD 4: COMPOSITION. GRADE 5 (ALL GENRES)

4.8.1.4   *Compose short pieces containing the appropriate elements of music*

Specific Knowledge

Understand basic rules of notation.

Performance Tasks

Compose or complete a simple four-to-eight-measure melody using given tones and/or rhythms.

4.8.2.4   *Arrange simple pieces for voices or instruments other than those for which the pieces were written.*

Specific Knowledge

Understand basic tonic and dominant chord changes.

Performance Tasks

Students arrange a simple one note accompaniment to a given or original melody using the root and fifth tones of the chord.

STANDARD 5: READING MUSIC. GRADE 6 BAND

5.8.1.6   *Read complex rhythms in simple and compound meters*

Specific Knowledge

Demonstrate an understanding of 2/4, 3/4, and 4/4 meters, using whole notes and rests through eighth notes and rests, including dotted-half and dotted-quarter notes and rests

Performance Tasks

Clap and count or play rhythms accurately using familiar or unfamiliar flash cards, exercises, or excerpts in current literature.

5.8.2.6   *Sightread simple melodies in both treble and bass clefs*

Specific Knowledge

In the appropriate clef, use knowledge of:

> steady beat
>
> rhythmic accuracy
>
> note recognitions
>
> fingerings

Performance Tasks

Students play accurate pitches in familiar and unfamiliar flash cards, exercises, or excerpts in current literature.

5.8.3.6 *Know standard notation symbols*

Specific Knowledge

Demonstrate, through writing or performance, an understanding of:

> key signatures
>
> accidentals
>
> 4/4, 3/4, and 2/4 meters

and have a fundamental understanding of:

> expression
>
> phrasing
>
> tempo changes
>
> interpretation of symbols, terms, and abbreviations appropriate to Level 1 music

Performance Tasks

Demonstrate how to read and label symbols and notes through worksheets providing definitions of musical symbols in Level 1 music.

STANDARD 6: LISTENING. GRADE 12 (ALL GENRES)

6.E.1.12 *Know the uses of the elements of music in the analysis of compositions representing diverse genres and cultures*

Specific Knowledge

Identify:

> musical elements
>
> Western and non-Western tonality
>
> Western and non-Western forms:
>
> fugue
>
> sonata
>
> theme and variations
>
> rondo

Performance Tasks

Analyze or describe elements of current repertoire. Listen to, compare, and contrast similar or contrasting styles of repertoire.

6.E.2.12   *Understand technical vocabulary of music*

Specific Knowledge

Identify and understand elements of:

music	harmony and form
tempo markings	articulations
English and non-English terms	

Performance Tasks

Construct an ongoing word bank to identify, discuss, or write elements of music using proper terminology.

STANDARD 7: EVALUATING MUSIC, GRADE 3 (ALL GENRES)

7.4.1.3   *Develop appropriate criteria to evaluate performances and compositions*

Specific Knowledge

Evaluate personal and group performance using grade-appropriate criteria and terminology

Performance Tasks

1. Develop three important criteria for evaluating music performances and compositions.
2. Write these criteria in the form of questions or descriptive phrases.
3. Listen to a recording or live performance, applying the above criteria in evaluations of the performance.

Specific Knowledge

Demonstrate respect for musical performances and opinions of others.

Performance Tasks

Listen respectfully and quietly to performers and show appropriate appreciation when performance is complete.

7.4.2.3   *Understand how to use music terminology to express personal preferences for specific musical works and styles*

Specific Knowledge

Use musical terminology to describe and support personal preference.

Performance Tasks

1. Share a favorite recording, explaining with appropriate terminology why the work is a favorite.
2. Choose instruments to accompany a melody, explaining with appropriate terminology why the instruments are chosen.

STANDARD 8: MUSIC AND OTHER DISCIPLINES. GRADE 6 (ALL GENRES)

8.8.1.6   *Know how relationships expressed through music can be expressed differently through other art disciplines*

Specific Knowledge

Understand how events or emotions can be expressed in other arts disciplines.

Examples:

thunderstorm	surprise
sunrise	excitement
sorrow	

Performance Tasks

Identify how at least one event, scene, emotion, or concept in music might also be represented in one of the other arts (e.g., theater, dance, or visual arts).

8.8.2.6   *Know how principles and concepts of other disciplines are related to those of music*

Specific Knowledge

Identify ways in which music is related to school subjects and daily life

Performance Tasks

Write one to two paragraphs identifying ways in which music is related to school subjects and used in daily life (e.g., sound production, movies, and television)

STANDARD 9: MUSIC, HISTORY, AND CULTURE. GRADE 10 (ALL GENRES)

9.E.1.10   *Know the representative examples of music from a variety of cultures and historical periods*

Specific Knowledge

Identify elements, composers, and musical examples of basic Western music history (e.g., Baroque, Classical, Romantic, Impressionistic, and Twentieth-century periods).

Performance Tasks

Prepare a report or presentation about a composition, describing its:

genre	composer
style	historical and cultural context
historical	period

9.E.2.10   *Know sources of American music, the evolution of these genres, and musicians associated with them*

Specific Knowledge

Know the history and styles of jazz (e.g., performers, composers, and characteristics

Performance Tasks
Listen to various styles of jazz and learn about the composers of each style. If possible, play examples.

9.E.3.10   ***Know the various roles that musicians perform and representative individuals who have functioned in each role***

Specific Knowledge
Study music careers/roles in history:

composer	teacher	publisher
performer	manager	sound technician
entertainer	editor	music therapist

Performance Tasks
Research and report on a career or musical role.

PERSONALIZING STANDARDS

Sometimes standards may pertain to district policies or areas that are important but not included in national or state standards.

Examples:
taking care of an instrument
tuning an instrument
technology application

Be aware that some writing across the curriculum or other district initiatives may need attention as its own standard or included within existing standards and benchmarks. When these are integrated into the curriculum, teachers can demonstrate to administrators that they are, first of all, aware of these initiatives and that they use them in their classrooms This is a very positive action which can only result in programs being taken seriously by the administration, other teachers, and parents.

STANDARD 10: UNDERSTAND HOW TO TAKE CARE OF AN INSTRUMENT. HIGH SCHOOL INSTRUMENTAL

10.E.1.10   *Demonstrate proper care of the instrument*

Specific Knowledge
Understand the monetary and aesthetic value of a step-up instrument and what qualities to look for when purchasing one.

Performance Tasks
Study the characteristics of a quality instrument and how to care for it.

Writing for Each Grade Level

Writing a standards document for each grade level is not only helpful for writing individual curriculum plans, but defines what is to be taught at each grade level.

Start with each set of standards and benchmarks grouped by K–4, grades 5–8, and 9–12. Specific knowledge and performance tasks can vary slightly, adding levels of difficulty.

ORCHESTRA EXAMPLE OF SPECIFIC KNOWLEDGE BY GRADE LEVEL

2.8.2   *Perform with expression and technical accuracy on a string, wind, percussion, or classroom instrument*

Grade 5

Demonstrate dynamic and tempo changes along with proper phrasing.

Perform with:

  proper posture

  position

  tone

  technique and style (which may include):

bow directions	two-to-three-note slurs	left-hand pizzicato
down bow	arco	staccato
up bow	pizzicato	legato

Grade 6

Demonstrate dynamic and tempo changes, along with proper phrasing.

Perform with:

  proper posture

  positions

  tone

  technique and style (which may include):

détaché	hooked bowings	accents
staccato	double stops	
two-to-four-note slurs	string crossings	

Grade 7

Demonstrate dynamic and tempo changes along with proper phrasing.

Perform with:

> proper posture
>
> positions
>
> tone
>
> technique and style (which may include):

détaché	four-to-eight-note slurs	string crossings	tremolo
marcato	hooked bowings	accents	
staccato	double stops	spiccato	

Grade 8

Demonstrate dynamic and tempo changes, along with proper phrasing, interpretation, and bow usage.

Perform with:

> proper posture
>
> positions
>
> tone
>
> technique and style (which may include):

détaché	hooked bowings	spiccato	sul tasto
marcato	double stops	tremolo	loure
staccato	string crossings	martelé	
four-to-eight-note slurs	accents	ponticello	

The beginning part of the specific knowledge can be the same but the "which may include" portion of the statement allows you to vary the levels of technique.

Specific knowledge can remain the same while performance levels for each grade can vary.

KNOWLEDGE BASE DOCUMENT BY GRADE

For each grade, a Knowledge Base document may be compiled from benchmark statements, specific knowledge, or performance tasks so that students know grade-level expectations for the year.

Music-writing programs (such as Finale and Sibelius) may be used to create music examples to be included in a Knowledge Base document. These programs allow staves to be positioned as needed and block text to be inserted anywhere.

Figure 2.

Grade 5 Knowledge Base for Double Bass, 2004

Double Bass

Grade 5 Knowledge Base 2004

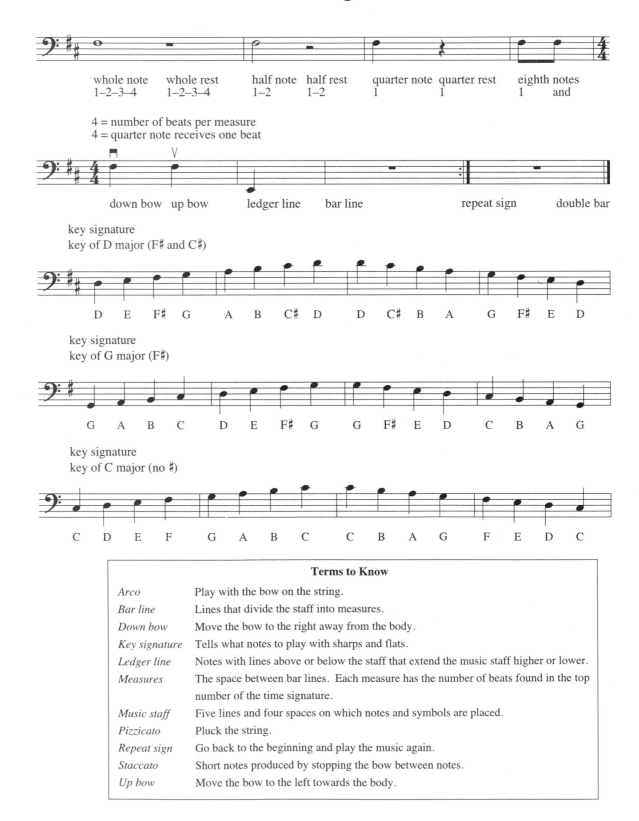

Terms to Know			
Arco	Play with the bow on the string.
Bar line	Lines that divide the staff into measures.
Down bow	Move the bow to the right away from the body.
Key signature	Tells what notes to play with sharps and flats.
Ledger line	Notes with lines above or below the staff that extend the music staff higher or lower.
Measures	The space between bar lines. Each measure has the number of beats found in the top number of the time signature.
Music staff	Five lines and four spaces on which notes and symbols are placed.
Pizzicato	Pluck the string.
Repeat sign	Go back to the beginning and play the music again.
Staccato	Short notes produced by stopping the bow between notes.
Up bow	Move the bow to the left towards the body.

Chapter 3

Suggested Performance Tasks or Activities for Each National Standard

As you write your curriculum, keep in mind some of the activities you can include for each standard. Several are listed below and may include some you may not have thought of before. You may add to this list as you write your curriculum.

STANDARD 1: SINGING. STUDENTS SING, ALONE AND WITH OTHERS, A VARIED REPERTOIRE OF MUSIC.

Elementary and Choral Music Classes

1. Sing:

folk songs	descants	marches	other part songs
rounds	counterparts	game songs	
ostinatos	partner songs	patriotic songs	

2. Sing songs or exercises using solfège.
3. Sightsing songs or intervals using solfège or note names.
4. Sing compositions written by self or others.
5. Record personal singing for assessment or portfolio.
6. Demonstrate emotion and expression through singing.
7. Demonstrate technique through singing.
8. Memorize a song.
9. Learn diction from songs in various languages.
10. Learn songs from different cultures.
11. Sing accompanied or *a cappella*.

12.   Sing call-and-response or question-and-answer statements.

13.   Sing scales and arpeggios.

14.   Sing melodies with kazoos.

15.   Sing many styles of music including:

jazz	rock
swing	music of composers of many different eras
gospel	

16.   Sing in parts.

Instrumental Classes

1.   Most folk songs beginners learn have words. Find words to these songs and have students sing them before or after they have learned to play them. Singing reinforces internal hearing and improves intonation.

2.   Hum and hold tuning pitches.

3.   Sing musical phrases before playing.

4.   Sing intervals.

5.   Sing call-and-response or question-and-answer statements.

6.   Sing the piece or excerpt using solfège.

7.   Demonstrate dynamics through singing, using a fixed pitch or a musical phrase.

8.   Demonstrate articulation through singing, using a fixed pitch or a musical phrase.

9.   Sing scales and arpeggios.

10.   Sing:

melodies	arpeggios
scales	melodic phrases using a voice or kazoo
chords	

STANDARD 2: INSTRUMENTAL PERFORMANCE. STUDENTS PERFORM ON INSTRUMENTS, ALONE AND WITH OTHERS, A VARIED REPERTOIRE OF MUSIC.

Elementary Music Classes

1.   Play a steady beat using body, rhythm instruments, or other objects.

2.   Demonstrate loud and soft, fast and slow, and short and long sounds on instruments.

3.   Play simple melodies on recorder or other pitched instruments.

4.   Play simple accompaniments on Orff or other pitched instruments.

5.   Learn to follow a conductor or a vocal group using rhythm or pitched instruments.

6.   Play scales, chords, and arpeggios using pitched rhythm instruments.

7.   Sightread rhythm cards using rhythm sticks, drums, or pitched rhythm instruments.

8.   Perform rhythmic and melodic ostinatos.

9.   Make instruments to practice rhythms or accompaniments.

10.   Play pieces in parts.

Choral Classes

1. Perform simple accompaniments on instruments for songs in class or performance.
2. Play scales, chords, and arpeggios using pitched rhythm instruments.
3. Sightread rhythm cards using rhythm sticks, drums, or pitched rhythm instruments.
4. Perform rhythmic and melodic ostinatos.
5. Make instruments to practice rhythms or accompaniments.

Instrumental Classes

1. Play scales, passages, phrases, lines, or pieces.
2. Play an accompaniment to a solo.
3. Play pieces in two or more parts.
4. Memorize a passage, phrase, line, or piece.
5. March or move while playing.
6. Play music of other cultures.
7. Play many styles of music including:

jazz	rock
swing	country
gospel	music of composers of many different eras

8. Demonstrate dynamics, tempos, and articulation through pieces.
9. Play pieces with varying tempos.
10. Perform in small and large groups.
11. Demonstrate technique through lines, phrases, and pieces.
12. Record individual and group performances.
13. Play a solo with or without accompaniment.

STANDARD 3: IMPROVISATION. STUDENTS IMPROVISE MELODIES, VARIATIONS, AND ACCOMPANIMENTS.

Elementary General Music, Choir, and Instrumental Music

1. Improvise a short phrase using given notes and rhythms.
2. Improvise a passage using notes in a given key signature or chord structure.
3. Improvise a rhythmic accompaniment.
4. Improvise an accompaniment using a given chord progression.
5. Improvise rhythmic and melodic variations on material already learned.
6. Improvise a rhythmic accompaniment using the body or other objects that make sound.
7. Improvise a melodic variation using neighboring tones on a given or original melody.
8. Improvise original melodies over a provided accompaniment.
9. Improvise vocally using scat or nonsense syllables.
10. Use the question-and-answer format to improvise an answer.
11. Improvise a passage using a set of newly learned notes.

STANDARD 4: COMPOSITION. STUDENTS COMPOSE AND ARRANGE MUSIC WITH SPECIFIED GUIDELINES.
Elementary General Music, Choir, and Instrumental Music

1. Compose ostinatos to known folk songs.
2. Write an ABA form composition using a variety of sources, such as poetry, folk songs, or a rhyme.
3. Compose rhythmic or melodic accompaniments using given notes, rhythms, or chord structures.
4. Compose a melody for a written text.
5. Compose a warm-up exercise in a given key with specific rhythms.
6. Compose a theme and variation using given or original material.
7. Compose or arrange various styles of music which may include:

jazz	blues
country	patriotic songs
classical	folk tunes from other countries or in the style of a piece or song already learned

8. Compose a piece for non-typical sound sources, such as environmental or electronic sounds.
9. Compose a piece in class in which each student is assigned a measure or phrase and then is constructed in the best possible order for performance.
10. Arrange a piece in a non-typical way, such as a patriotic song converted into a blues song.
11. Arrange a piece using specific instrumental accompaniment.
12. Arrange a piece using a specific form.
13. Arrange an accompaniment to an existing or composed melody.

STANDARD 5: READING MUSIC. STUDENTS READ AND NOTATE MUSIC
Elementary General Music, Choir, and Instrumental Music

1. Read and notate symbols, notes, expression marks, and tempo settings.
2. Clap, count, or play rhythms in familiar or unfamiliar flashcards, exercises, or excerpts.
3. Play pitches in familiar or unfamiliar flashcards, exercises, or excerpts.
4. Label notes, rhythms, or intervals.
5. Demonstrate how to notate symbols and placement of notes and rhythms.
6. Read scores, recognizing melody lines, chord progressions, modulations, or form.
7. Transpose excerpts of music.
8. Sightread examples using familiar notation, key signatures, and rhythms.
9. Write rhythmic or melodic dictation.
10. Know notes from various clefs.
11. Demonstrate dynamic or tempo markings through music reading.
12. In an unfamiliar piece of music, create a scavenger hunt to find symbols, tempo changes, accidentals, new rhythms, or new notes.
13. Create a practice guide in which students identify and explain new symbols, key signatures, or terms found in a new piece of music.

STANDARD 6: LISTENING. STUDENTS LISTEN TO, ANALYZE, AND DESCRIBE MUSIC.

Elementary General Music, Choir, and Instrumental Music

1. Listen to and identify different forms of music such as ABA, fugue, or concerto.
2. Listen to and identify music of different cultures, including our own.
3. Listen to and identify different styles of music such as:

Broadway musicals	twelve-tone
jazz	marching band
blues	

4. Listen to and identify instruments in listening exercises.
5. Listen to and identify composers in listening exercises.
6. Create a word bank of music terms and definitions that can be accessed when listening to, analyzing, or describing music.
7. Identify major or minor tonality in listening exercises.
8. Identify elements of music such as:

timbre	retrograde	modulation
motif	chromaticism	major or minor tonality
inversion	key changes	

9. Compare and contrast sections of music.
10. Compare and contrast two different recordings of a piece or recordings of it by your school group and a professional group.
11. Record a school performance and analyze and describe the performance using a word bank. Include aspects that were done well and those that need improvement. Did students follow the conductor, dynamic markings, phrase markings, and "road map" markings?
12. Analyze the performance of solos and ensembles in class or at performances.
13. Demonstrate personal interpretations of recorded or live music through movement.
14. Conduct a recorded or live musical example demonstrating dynamics and articulation

STANDARD 7: EVALUATING MUSIC. STUDENTS EVALUATE MUSIC AND MUSIC PERFORMANCE.

Elementary General Music, Choir, and Instrumental Music

1. Evaluate the performance of others using a rubric of given criteria and/or word bank of correct terms. Include:

musical expression	blend
technique	interpretation of musical symbols
intonation	balance and communication of group

2. Demonstrate respect for performers or a performing group.
3. Write a personal reaction to a specific performance.
4. Define appropriate and inappropriate feedback when evaluating the performance of others.

5. Evaluate self after an assessment. What went well? What can be improved?

6. Evaluate the aesthetic value of a piece.

7. Understand how to receive feedback from others.

8. Listen to a musical example and decide how to market it to an audience.

STANDARD 8: MUSIC AND OTHER DISCIPLINES. STUDENTS UNDERSTAND THE RELATIONSHIP BETWEEN MUSIC, THE OTHER ARTS, AND OTHER DISCIPLINES.

Elementary General Music, Choir, and Instrumental Music

1. Demonstrate how concepts in music such as:

unity	color
texture	tone
line	

   are found in:

music	dance
literature	theater arts
visual art	

2. Examine how music has expressed history during times of war, slavery, or peace.

3. Know how music is reflected in world events such as the Olympics or advertising.

4. Identify how emotions are portrayed in music, theater, dance, visual arts, and literature.

5. Relate rhythm to fractions.

6. Relate terms to languages.

7. Relate sound production to science and physics.

8. Relate musical eras to history. What else occurred around the world when Bach lived regarding:

inventions	wars
literature	historical events

9. Relate written evaluations of music to Language Arts using Six Traits Writing.

10. Compare academic test scores of musician students to non-musician students.

11. Compare and contrast a concept in music, visual arts, theater arts, dance and literature. Examples:

play	symphony
musical	art display
opera	

12. Know roles of creators, performers, and others involved in the production and presentation of the arts:

writer	casting agent	cinematographers
composer	performer	
technician	animator	

13. Identify settings for various musical happenings such as:

symphony concerts	pow-wows	jam sessions
rock concerts	square dances	
musicals	school concerts	

STANDARD 9: MUSIC, HISTORY, AND CULTURE. STUDENTS UNDERSTAND MUSIC IN RELATION TO HISTORY AND CULTURE.

Elementary General Music, Choir, and Instrumental Music

1. Examine how music has expressed history during times of war, slavery, or peace.
2. Relate musical eras to what else was a part of the world when Bach, lived such as:

inventions	trends
wars	fashion
famous people	events

3. Find similarities in the ways we express ourselves in various cultures, such as music, dance, and art.
4. Recognize characteristics of music from different cultures.
5. Compare and contrast two musical selections from two different cultures, countries, or eras of music.
6. Analyze music of different cultures.
7. Create a new culture, taking best practices from several varying cultures.
8. Recognize characteristics of music from various eras.
9. Observe different cultural rituals.
10. Identify why a certain musical genre is from a specific period of music.
11. Create a list of musical excerpts that students should be able to identify, such as famous pieces from different genres, the National Anthem, or other patriotic selections.

CONCERT IDEAS

Standards may be addressed through concerts. Parents and administrators become more aware of our music standards when you communicate them at a public event. This strengthens your music program as a viable core subject.

A Taste of Music Concert, Standard 9: MUSIC, HISTORY, AND CULTURE

Creating a theme for a concert is a great idea that opens the door for involving families or other students in your concert. It also creates an awareness of music standards.

Start the year with *A Taste of Music* concert with hors d'œurve in the cafeteria prior to the concert of music from all nationalities.

1. For ideas for food and decorations, enlist the help of:

    foreign exchange students

    English language learners

    families of varying cultures

    foreign-language teachers

    This theme ties in nicely with Standard 9 (Understanding music in relation to history and culture).

2. Send home a letter to parents describing the concert and requesting food and decoration contributions.

3. Contact area businesses for food donations or decorations in exchange for advertising in the program.

4. Purchase colorful plastic tablecloths and paper placemats to transform the cafeteria into a festive restaurant.

5. Ask students to create flags from various countries to hang in the cafeteria or auditorium.

Here are the partnerships that develop:

1. Parents become involved in their child's musical activity.

2. Parents of music students new to the school start the year with a positive experience and become involved right at the start of the year.

3. Area businesses see first-hand what is happening in public school music programs. They can contribute food or decorations in exchange for advertising in the program.

4. English language learners, foreign exchange students and foreign-language teachers get a chance to share their culture with others. This allows English language learners to make a new connection to students at school and share their culture with others.

5. Students have time to socialize before and after the concert with set-up and clean-up.

6. Don't forget to write thank-you notes to parents, businesses, and other people involved immediately after the program.

Music in Our Schools Month, Standard 9: MUSIC, HISTORY, AND CULTURE

March is Music in Our Schools Month. Play or sing a joint concert with a musical group that will be attending your school the following year. Play or sing pieces by composers born in March, such as:

Vivaldi	Rimsky-Korsakov
Smetana	Ravel
Bach	Haydn

Create a PowerPoint presentation with pictures of and information on the composers and eras in which they composed, what else may occurred around the world then, and references used.

Special outcomes of this type of concert:
1. Music in our Schools Month publicity.
2. Younger students connect with the new school and teacher for next year.
3. Parents are educated about music by viewing the presentation.
   Include music advocacy statements at the end of the presentation or during the program.
4. Play or sing music from all eras of music.
5. Standard 1: SINGING, Standard 2: INSTRUMENTAL PERFORMANCE, Standard 5: READING MUSIC, and Standard 9: MUSIC, HISTORY, AND CULTURE are addressed.
6. Students help each other with designing the PowerPoint presentation.

Academy Award Concert Theme, Standard 8: MUSIC AND OTHER DISCIPLINES
Select movie themes to create an Academy Awards theme concert.
1. Have hor d'oeurves before the concert.
2. Install a red carpet and ropes (sometimes found in the cafeteria) to put at the entrance of the school.
3. Ask limo companies to donate free rides before the concert.
4. If awards are presented at the last concert of the year, incorporate this into the theme.
5. Invite an area newscaster or district superintendent to be the master of ceremonies to introduce pieces.
6. Create a PowerPoint presentation showing pictures or film clips to go along with movie themes. Be aware of copyright laws when doing this.
7. Using a projector, trace and cut out several eight-foot award statues, spray paint them gold and hang them in the cafeteria during hor d'oeurves.
8. For a "Walk of Fame," cut out stars, mount on black paper, and write the name of each student on them. These can be put in a row across the front of the stage, around the auditorium, or another visible location.
9. Include ads or thank-yous in the program for companies donating food, drinks, limo rides, or red carpets.
10. Thank these companies in writing after the concert as well.
11. Ask parents to contribute food and decorations.
12. This concert ties in with Standard 8: MUSIC AND OTHER DISCIPLINES.

Chapter 4

Sequencing Method Books, Literature, Theory, and Teaching Aids

Some teaching materials have changed to address national standards but don't always fulfill all needs of the district curriculum. Supplementary materials need to be added when using textbooks or method books so that your curriculum is complete.

Add to your teaching resources each year, using a portion of your budget, money from the Parent Teacher Association, or grants. The school library can purchase books and DVDs for your use. It is evident that this enhances teaching and is well worth the extra time to write requests or grants.

CHOOSING APPROPRIATE TEACHING MATERIALS

Items that assist in teaching concepts to students who are aural, visual, or kinesthetic learners:

1. Method books.
2. Textbooks.
3. Projectors to show computer files or materials.
4. DVDs or videos.
5. CDs.
6. Computer programs for composition, theory, history, composers, or styles of music.
7. A list of websites for theory or history.
8. Resource books from the library or purchased on your own.
9. Flash cards (homemade or purchased).
10. Tactile equipment such as popsicle sticks for rhythmic dictation.
11. Music games (homemade or purchased).
12. Worksheets.
13. Audio equipment for listening and recording.

14.   Photos or posters of instruments, composers, solfège hand signs, diction, etc.

15.   Educational and motivational bulletin boards.

16.   Posters of the nine national music standards in your room.

17.   Laminated sets of rubrics for the class used for assessment.

18.   Pitched and non-pitched instruments.

19.   Staff paper.

20.   A magnetic whiteboard with staff lines.

21.   Magnetic noteheads and symbols to go with the whiteboard.

22.   Staff lines taped on the floor and bean bags or plastic noteheads.

23.   Staff lines painted or pre-manufactured on the whiteboard.

24.   Individual whiteboards for notation and dictation.

25.   A classroom set of colored pencils for circling intervals, symbols, or concepts in music.

26.   Small percussion equipment, such as rhythm sticks, Orff instruments, bells, etc.

27.   Kazoos.

28.   Recorders.

29.   Learning centers or packets for listening or history.

FORMATTING ACTIVITIES, MATERIALS, AND RESOURCES TO FIT THE STANDARDS-BASED CURRICULUM

It is best to find materials that address concepts in the standards instead of selecting a textbook or method book and going from cover to cover. Textbooks are becoming a resource from which we select what we want to teach and when.

As you write your curriculum, draw ideas from textbooks or method books to create a list of activities for each standard. Add resource materials present in your classroom to the list as well.

By listing activities and materials or resources needed for them, you can take inventory of current teaching supplies and fill gaps for standards that need more resources or activities. Students like and need a variety of learning activities, and increasing the volume and variety of tools assists visual, tactile, and aural learners' ability to understand concepts.

Organize individual activities in a detailed format that can be created on a spreadsheet for each activity done in the classroom with the following format:

Figure 3.
Formatting Activities Form

Course _____ Grade _____

Concept _____

Standard(s) used (circle all that apply)					
Sing	1	Perform	2	Improvise	3
Compose	4	Arrange	4	Reading music	5
Notating music	5	Listening	6	Analyzing	7
Evaluating	7	Relationship to other arts/subjects	8	Culture	9
History	9				

Benchmark number	Benchmark Description

Steps	
Specific Knowledge/ Learning Target(s)	
Assessment	
Performance Tasks (Activities)	
Materials/Resources	

First determine your learning target or goal. What do you want students to learn? Next write your assessment(s). Creating assessments before writing activities establishes a clear path to achieving your learning targets. All teachers have had great activities at some point and then realized later that assessments and activities don't match learning targets. Sometimes assessments cannot be easily implemented if written after activities are set.

Design assessments and activities that include more than one standard or benchmark (referred to as chunking). This is an efficient way to cover material, as several assessments may be used for evidence of understanding or learning.

For example, steps for a beginning instrumental class might be:

Figure 4.

Example of Chunking Standards

Standard(s) used (circle all that apply):

Sing (1)	Perform (2)	Improvise (3)
Compose (4)	Arrange (4)	Reading music (5)
Notating music (5)	Listening (6)	Analyzing (7)
Evaluating (7)	Relationship to other arts/subjects (8)	Culture (9)
History (9)		

Benchmark	Description
1.8.1	Sing accurately and with good breath control throughout their singing ranges, alone and in small and large groups.
2.8.1	Perform on an instrument, alone and in small and large groups.
3.8.2	Improvise melodic embellishments and simple rhythmic and melodic variations.
4.8.1	Compose short pieces containing the appropriate elements of music.
5.8.2	Sightread simple melodies in both the treble and bass clefs.

Steps	
Specific Knowledge/Learning Target(s)	Learn new notes B-flat, A and G
Assessment	1. Students individually vocally match pitches of B-flat, A, and G.
	2. Students individually perform exercise 24.
	3. Students individually improvise B-flat, A, and G with the rhythms found in exercise 24.
	4. Check composition for correct notes and rhythms along with note and stem placement.
	5. Students assess another student's composition.
Performance Tasks (Activities)	1. Students sing the pitches B-flat, A, and G correctly repeating the order of notes sung by the teacher.
	2. Students play exercise 24 together using B-flat, A, and G until mastered.
	3. Students improvise a two measure phrase using B-flat, A, and G and the rhythms in exercise 24.
	4. Students compose a four measure exercise using B-flat, A and G and the same rhythms found in exercise 24.
	5. Students play their own composition and then trade with a neighbor to play their composition and make corrections if needed.
Materials/Resources	1. Method book exercise 24.
	2. Composition paper and pencils.
	3. Composition rubric.
	4. Improvisation rubric.
	5. Performance rubric.

SEQUENCING METHOD OR TEXTBOOKS (STANDARDS-BASED ACTIVITIES)

Because you are using a textbook or method book as a resource, it is necessary to go through these and identify concepts for each exercise, song, or piece. After this is completed, add activities that enhance songs, such as analysis, composition, improvisation, listening, or evaluation.

Use a spreadsheet program (such as Microsoft Excel or the free Google Docs software, available at docs. google.com/) to set up a form for sequencing method books.

1. Set up the spreadsheet in landscape view (the paper is wide).

2. List the following items in the first row. (Note: This list may span two pages.)

    a. Page

    b. Name of piece or song

    c. Key signature (Standard 5)

    d. Notes used when new notes are introduced (Standard 5)

    e. Rhythms used when rhythms are introduced (Standard 5)

    f. Articulation

        Examples: staccato, legato, or phrasing (Standard 5)

    g. Dynamics (Standard 5)

    h. Sing words, solfège, phrases, lines, or exercises (Standard 1)

    i. Play a line, phrase, song, exercise, or accompaniment (Standard 2)

    j. Improvisation

        Example: start a phrase from this piece but improvise an ending

        improvise using a set of notes or rhythms from the piece (Standard 3)

    k. Composition

        Example: write a composition or accompaniment to correspond with this piece
              (Standard 4)

    l. Form (Standard 6)

    m. Listen (Standard 6)

    n. Evaluate (Standard 7)

    o. Ensemble

        Examples: performing in parts, ostinato, or internal partner song (Standard 1 or 2)

    p. Transposition

        Example: transpose a line or phrase of a piece (Standard 4)

    q. Relation to other music and disciplines (Standard 8)

    r. Culture

        Example: discuss any cultural characteristics of this piece (Standard 9)

    s. History

        Example: discuss any historical details of the piece (Standard 9)

3. Include activities to enhance learning a song, piece, or exercise. It is important to keep the list of standards in view to make sure you use all standards at some point in lesson planning. Standard 5 is listed before the others because sequencing often involves certain note and rhythm sequences before anything else.

Figure 5.

Method Book Sequencing Form

Name of Text or Method Book:

Standard		5	5	5	5	5	7	2	3	4	5	6	7	8	9	9
	Piece or page	Key Signature	Notes Used	Rhythms Used	Articulations	Form	Ensemble	Improv	Composition	Transposition	Listening	Evaluate	Other Subjects	Culture	History

Document the textbook or method book from beginning to end. Your sequence of concepts to be taught may differ from what is presented in these books. You may even find you like to use more than one method book or textbook, selecting what is to be taught when through the course of the year.

Some instrumental teachers prefer to teach everything in a particular key with graduated rhythms before going on to another key. Other teachers may approach the curriculum by having a quick overview of key signatures and then going back and studying material in each key in depth.

Having improvisation, composition, form, ensemble, transposition, relation to other music and disciplines, culture, and history on the form, serves as a reminder to incorporate these standards into curriculum planning.

There is no definite answer concerning how often to teach each standard, but blending all of them into the curriculum enhances knowledge and depth of student understanding.

Once you have sequenced all of the materials to use in the classroom, create a syllabus (see chapter 5). If sequencing by key signature and rhythm, the page numbers and your textbook or method book may not match the order of your syllabus. There may be frequent changing of books to accommodate practice of a skill or concept.

A good idea in upper grades is to use technique books for warm-up, solo literature materials, and then material featuring playing in parts in each key. This is a nice exposure to many facets of playing or singing in an organized manner.

DOCUMENTING LITERATURE

For each piece of performance literature in your library, complete information about the piece so that each time you use it you have a rehearsal plan in mind.

Detailing the key signature, level of difficulty, technical challenges, and other issues that may occur in the piece may take a bit of time initially, but will save time in the future. For example, each time you play a piece, decisions have already been made for the warm-up, what vocabulary the students need to know, and what particular areas need attention in the piece.

Figure 6.
Literature Detail Inventory Form

Title of composition _____	
Composer_____	
Level of difficulty_____	

Focus: what benchmark expectation

Key	Accidentals	Meter	Roadmap	Anything unusual
Warm-up to be used				

Rhythms used
Intonation/pitch issues
Technical issues
Word bank
Precision rehearsal areas
Phrasing and expression areas
Balance and blend areas

Chapter 5

Designing an Organized Curriculum

CREATING A LOGICAL ORDER

At this point, conclusions can be made as to what to teach and when by drawing from the lists of materials, activities and resources, and sequencing method books. Elementary music teachers like to teach songs in a certain solfège and rhythm sequence. Choral instructors like to teach songs in certain voice ranges at particular ages. Instrumental teachers need to start with particular finger patterns and rhythms. Every teacher has individual thoughts on these subjects.

FORMAT

Begin to create a sequenced list using a format such as the one in figure 7. Again, set up a spreadsheet in landscape mode to accomplish this. If there is more than one section or class using the same curriculum, add section numbers at the top of the list at the end of the spreadsheet. Mark these with an X in the section/class column when the activity is completed. This clearly indicates what has or has not been accomplished with each section when lesson plans are written. Some classes may take longer on a project or task than others.

An organized curriculum labels the introduction of new concepts, review or practice of new concepts, activities from the standards-based activity list, and assessments. Under the last part of the grid are section or class numbers. In this example, class sections A4 and B4 completed the first listing but only class A4 completed the second listing.

Figure 7.

Classroom Sequenced Syllabus or Curriculum Guide

BOOK	PAGE	TUNE/ACTIVITY	KEY	ASSESS	RHYTHM	A4	B4	A7	B7	A8	B8
ET	22–23	scale/arppeggio	D	Yes							
ST	17	In the Country	D		dotted notes						
ST	20	Child's Prayer	D		dotted notes						
ST	24	Classic March, G. F. Handel	D		dotted notes						
Learn about the composer G. F. Handel and listen to excerpts of his music.											
HR	2		D								
HR	4		D	Yes							
WK	1, 4	dotted quarters/eighths			dotted notes						
HR	5		D		dotted notes						
HR	7		D		eighths/dotted quarters						
HR	25		D		sixteenths						
HR	31		D		dotted eighths						
ET	3, 4	pages 7–13, III	D								
Fingercharts											
Write the D major scale on the scale packet.											
Build the D major scale with flashcards.											
Improvise on D tetrachords/scale/arpeggios											
Compose an eight-measure piece in the key of D using dotted-quarter and eighth notes.				Yes							
ET	20–21	scale/arpeggio/third	G	Yes							
ST	6	Minuet No. 1, J. S. Bach	G								
ST	9	March, J. S. Bach	G		tied notes						
Learn about the composer J. S. Bach and listen to excerpts of his music.											
ST	13	Gavotte, F. J. Gossec	G								
ST	14–15	Theme and Variations, Guido Papini	G	Yes							
Listen to another theme and variations.											
Learn metric and melodic variation strategies.											
Compose a theme and variations based on a four-measure theme in the key of G.											
ST	16	Heroic March, G. F. Handel	G		dotted notes						
Play page 24, Classic March. Compare and contrast with ST page 9, March by J. S. Bach.											
ST	17	Happy Farmer, Robert Schumann	G		dotted notes						

Figure 7. (continued)
Classroom Sequenced Syllabus or Curriculum Guide

BOOK	PAGE	TUNE/ACTIVITY	KEY	ASSESS	RHYTHM	A4	B4	A7	B7	A8	B8
HR	1	Learn about the composer Robert Schumann and listen to excerpts of his music.	G								
HR	19		G		sixteenths						
ER	4, 5	pages 14–18, III/IV	G								
HR	30		G		dotted eighths						
ST	2	*Famous Melodies*, Antonín Dvořák	G								
ET	2	pages 1–6, III	G/g								
ST	5	*Melodies*, Frédéric Chopin	G		dotted eighths						
		Write the G scale on the scale packet.									
		Build the G major scale with flashcards.									
		Improvise on the G major arpeggio with rhythmic accompaniment (use electric piano).									
		Compose an eight-measure warm-up in G using quarter and eighth notes.									
		Rhythm flash game: "Who's Got?" (quarter and eighth notes).									
ET	18–19	scale/arpeggio/third	C								
ST	1	*The Surprise Symphony*, Franz Joseph Haydn	C								
		Learn about Franz Joseph Haydn.									
		Listen to *The Surprise Symphony* by Franz Joseph Haydn.									
ST	2	*Symphony No. 1*, Johannes Brahms	C								
		Learn about the composer Johannes Brahms.									
ST	19	*Ave Verum Corpus*, W. A. Mozart	C								
		Learn about the composer W. A. Mozart and listen to excerpts of his music.									
HR	26		C	Yes	sixteenths						
		I've Got Rhythm, pages 5–7			dotted notes						
		HS, WS, and enharmonics		Yes								
		Write the C Scale.									
		Build the C major scale with flashcards.									
		Compose an eight-to-twelve-measure warm-up using sixteenth notes and transpose it to D.									
ET	26–27		F								

Figure 7. (continued)

Classroom Sequenced Syllabus or Curriculum Guide

BOOK	PAGE	TUNE/ACTIVITY	KEY	ASSESS	RHYTHM	A4	B4	A7	B7	A8	B8
ST	1	Minuet, Franz Joseph Haydn	F								
ST	3	Country Song, Ludwig van Beethoven	F		dotted notes						
		Learn about the composer Ludwig van Beethoven and listen to excerpts of his music.									
ST	4	Symphony No. 4, P. I. Tchaikovsky	F								
		Learn about the composer P. I. Tchaikovsky and listen to excerpts of his music.									
ST	7	Melody in F, Anto Rubenstein	F								
ST	8	Minuet, J. S. Bach	F								
ST	21	Love is Kind/Londondery Air	F								
HR	3		F								
HR	20		F	Yes	dotted notes						
		I've Got Rhythm, pages 8–10									
HR	22		F		sixteenths						
HR	29		F		dotted eighths						
HR	8		F	Yes	dotted notes						
		I've Got Rhythm, pages 11–12									
HR	9		F		syncopated						
		Rhythm flash game: "Who's Got?"			syncopated						
HR	33		F		dotted eighths						
		Write the F major scale.									
		Build the F major scale with flashcards.									
		Watch the Music Is Composed video.									
		Write an eight-to-twelve-measure composition in the key of F using syncopated rhythms.									
ET	28–29		B-flat								
ST	11	Christmas tunes	B-flat								
HR	6		B-flat		dotted notes						
HR	23		B-flat	Yes							
		I've Got Rhythm, pages 13–14			sixteenths						

Figure 7. (continued)

Classroom Sequenced Syllabus or Curriculum Guide

BOOK	PAGE	TUNE/ACTIVITY	KEY	ASSESS	RHYTHM	A4	B4	A7	B7	A8	B8
HR	21		B-flat		sixteenths						
HR	28		B-flat		dotted eighths						
HR	9		B-flat		syncopated						
HR	33		B-flat		dotted eighths						
HR	24		B-flat	Yes	eighths/ sixteenths						
		I've Got Rhythm, page 15									
		Write the B-flat major scale.									
		Build the B-flat major scale with flashcards.									
		Computer lab: Work with CD-ROMs on composers									
HR	10		D	Yes	6/8 meter						
		I've Got Rhythm, page 16									
HR	12		D		12/8 meter						
HR	13		D		9/8 meter						
HR	18		D		12/8 meter						
HR	38		D		3/8 meter						
HR	41		D		6/8 meter						
		Key signature workbook									
ST	12	Larghetto, G. F. Handel	G		6/8 meter						
HR	15		G		6/8 meter						
HR	16		G		9/8 meter						
HR	37		G		6/8 meter						
		Flashcards: note types and beats		Yes							
		Workbook, page 34		Yes							
		Workbook, page 32		Yes							
ST	18	Barcarolle, Jacques Offenbach	C								
		Learn about the composer Jacques Offenbach and listen to excerpts of his music.									
		Listen to Orpheus in the Underworld.									
HR	11		C		6/8 meter						

Figure 7. (continued)

Classroom Sequenced Syllabus or Curriculum Guide

BOOK	PAGE	TUNE/ACTIVITY	KEY	ASSESS	RHYTHM	A4	B4	A7	B7	A8	B8
HR	14		C		9/8 meter						
HR	17		C		6/8 meter						
		Workbook, scale pitches, page 23									
		Write a warm-up in D, G, C, F, or B-flat in 6/8 meter.									
ET	30–31		E-flat								
HR	42		G		5/8 meter						
HR	44		G		5/8 meter						
ST	22	Franz Schubert	G/g								
ET	19–33	Harmonics	C/D/G/A								
ET	7 to 8	36–42									
ET	41	spiccato	C/D/G								
ET	44	trill	D								

ELEMENTARY GENERAL MUSIC CURRICULUM EXAMPLE

Elementary general music teachers may compile a curriculum overview (or mapping) which becomes a syllabus or curriculum guide. This is a list of songs to be learned, what to prepare, present, and practice, and what rhythm and melody sequence to use in a Kodály-based classroom. A curriculum guide can be established from this plan with the sequence of what to teach when.

In an elementary standards-based curriculum that is not Kodály-based, the syllabus may look more like the example in figure 9.

The use of composition and improvisation allow students to practice new concepts in different ways than singing which reinforces what students have learned. Listening to the mi-re-do sequence in a recording assists students in recognizing the pattern aurally. Singing or listening to the pattern in different settings, such as a vocal piece and a symphony, demonstrates to students that this sequence is used in many different genres. By using varying techniques, students are engaged, they practice a concept in a variety of ways and it allows the teacher to incorporate many different standards and apply quick assessments.

Figure 8.

Grade 4: September/October of Year Plan

Two Classes per Week at Thirty Minutes Each

Month	Song Material	Prepare	Present	Practice	Rhythm	Melody
SEPTEMBER	1. Yankee Doodle (movement and sing) 2. Conduct *Rocky Mountain* 3. *To Stop the Train* 4. Poems with and without anacrusis 5. *I Can Do the Tap Dance* 6. *I've Got to Rise* 7. *Alabama Gal* with *Way Down South* poem 8. *It Rained on Ann* 9. *Hello Everybody* 10. Flower Chart with rhythms 11. *Cairo* 12. *Are You Sleeping* 13. <u>*I Got a Letter*</u> 14. *Fishpole* 15. *Turn Glasses Over* 16. *Jubilee*	Movement exploration with poetry/levels Facing, direction Syncopa Low *sol-la* visually/aurally	Anacrusis	Beat/Rhythm: *du, du-de* *rests* *halfs* *dotted halfs* Meter: 4/4 3/4 2/4 Phrase: Q/A Form: *aaab* *aaba* *abab* Pentatonic	1. Move, Sing, Play BEAT and RHYTHM 2. Read rhythm cards 3. Improvise eight-beat phrase with ♩♪ 𝅘𝅥𝅯 4. Eight-beat rhythm ostinato 5. Passing games with anacrusis 6. Movement and conducting with anacrusis 7. Hip/hup subdivision with movement	1. Singing Voice: vocal exploration 2. Solfège echoes with entire pentatonic using s, l, drmsl 3. Draw icons for low *la-sol* and label 4. Aurally ID low *la* and *sol* in songs 5. Body solfège
OCTOBER	1. *Canoe Song* 2. *Brickyard*: recorders 3. *Cairo*: recorders 4. *Gilly Gilly* 5. *Who Killed Cock Robin*: ID as la-based 6. Movement with partner to "Pier Gynt": *Hall of the Mountain King* 7. *Peace Canon* 8. *It Rained on Ann*: recorders 9. *I've Got to Rise* 10. *Alabama Gal* 11. Flower rhythm chart 12. *I Don't Care if the Rain…* 13. *Hop Up and Jump Up* (363) 14. *Sourwood Mountain* (196)	Aurally prep high *do*	Low *la* and *sol* Syncopa	Solfège with *fa* *p*, *f*, fermata through movement Form: call-and-response AB Crescendo/decrescendo and dynamics 3/4 meter	1. Compose and conduct in 3/4 2. Decipher mystery rhythms with short-long-short 3. Alter eighths in *Dance* to *du-ta-de* or *du-de-ta* 4. RU w/syncopa	1. Echo solfège with low *la* and *sol*: decipher at instruments 2. Locate d' on body 3. Write l, s, on staff: read in known songs 4. Beach Ball staff notation (l, s) 5. Floor staff: st. bounce as class sings known song by solfa 6. Play low *la* and *sol* on recorder

Figure 9.

Grade 3: Year Plan

Four Classes per Week at Twenty-five Minutes Each

Source	Page	Introduce	Practice	Rhythm	Melody	Activity	Assessment	1–1	1–2	1–3	1–4
Name of text	25	mi, re, do	mi, re, do	[musical notation]	mi, re, do B—A—G	Sing song using solfège and then words	Each student vocally matches mi, re, do individually	x	x	x	x
Name of text	13		mi, re, do	[musical notation]	mi, re, do B—A—G	Sing song using solfège and then words	Each student vocally matches a phrase of the song after the teacher's example	x	x	x	
Finale Notepad		Finale Notepad	Finale Notepad	[musical notation]	mi, re, do B—A—G	Compose an eight-beat phrase using [musical notation]	Correct placement of mi, re, do and correct rhythms	x			
			mi, re, do	[musical notation]	mi, re, do B—A—G	Improvise an eight-beat phrase using mi, re, do and [musical notation]	Correct use of pitch, rhythms and number of beats in the phrase				
Hot Cross Buns			mi, re, do	[musical notation]	mi, re, do B—A—G	Play on the recorder	Individual performance of Hot Cross Buns				
Recording			mi, re, do	[musical notation]	mi, re, do B—A—G	Listen to two contrasting recordings of songs that contain mi, re, do and have students raise hands as they hear mi, re, do	Quickly assess students as they raise their hands				

x = class has completed task

Chapter 6

Lesson Plans

To review the process so far, think of it as a trickle-down effect:
1.   MENC standards (targets grades 4–8 and 12)
2.   State standards (can be adapted to fit the needs of each state)
3.   District standards (can be broken down into grade level and genre)
4.   Individual curriculum (syllabus which includes the sequenced materials that are used to teach district standards)

The focus now becomes writing daily lesson plans based on the individual curriculum or syllabus. Always plan more than you will need so if a class moves quickly through the lesson, you will be prepared to offer more material.

Music educators are faced with the need to teach a spiraling curriculum as well as produce a product—the concert. If your standards-based curriculum is carefully constructed by grade level and genre, you will successfully create a quality curriculum that spirals up through the grades.

Some concepts are taught at several grade levels but are more in depth in upper grades. Listing all concepts to be covered by grade level allows you to have a complete picture of what is taught when and makes writing lesson plans easy. This is especially nice for new teachers in a district to review before starting their first year of teaching.

Having the district curriculum in place allows freedom to use materials that work best for individual teachers, whether method books, performance literature, or both. The important issue is that all teachers cover the elements of the district curriculum. All teachers know that concert dates occasionally prohibit covering material thoroughly. One way to avoid this problem is to incorporate the knowledge base concepts into performance material. If dotted-quarter notes or syncopated rhythms need to be addressed, find pieces for your concert that contain these rhythms.

General education is moving away from starting at the beginning of a textbook and finishing it by the end of the school year. Music teachers should also review how a method book is sequenced, perhaps change the order taught, and supplement when necessary. Beginning instrumental method books are usually thoughtfully sequenced, but after a couple of years of instruction, it becomes necessary to find a variety of materials and sequence them according to the curriculum. General music books may cover a lot of standards-based materials, but it is up to the teacher to sequence what is taught when and supplement when necessary.

Whether teaching general, instrumental, or choral music, warm-ups are always a great way to start a class period and focus student attention on music. This could be practicing something previously learned or an introduction to a new concept. In-depth practice should be in the middle of class, and the end of class should be a run-through of a piece or an activity students enjoy.

Planning lessons from day to day is important to the success of teaching. Notice in the syllabus in chapter 5 that the different class sections are listed at the end of the chart. By documenting the progress of each class and referring to it as the lesson plans are written, all class sections can work at their own pace.

WHAT TO INCLUDE IN A LESSON PLAN BOOK

Purchase a three-ring binder that has clear pockets on the outside. Insert your schedule into the front cover pocket. Divide inside sections into:

1. Attendance policies and procedures
2. Class lists
3. Names of students in each section that can be trusted to assist with class
3. Lesson plans
4. Tuning procedures (instrumental)
5. Syllabus
6. Special lists of students with medical or special needs
7. Quick assessment lists with students' names in alphabetical order for tracking who has returned forms, assignments, payments, etc., or specific quick assessment documentation
8. Emergency plans for lock-downs, tornado, fire, evacuations, etc.
9. Instrument and music storage charts
10. Substitute teacher feedback forms

LESSON PLAN EXAMPLES

Figure 10.

Orchestra Lesson Plan Page

Day A or B	DAY: M T W TH F	Date			
Period	**Class**	**Time**	**Warm-up**	**Literature**	**Activity**
A1	8th Teal Orchestra	7:55–8:40			
B1	Grade 8 black orchestra	7:55–8:40			
Period 1	Grade 8 chamber orchestra	7:55–8:40			
Friday					
A2/B2	Channel 1/Advisory	8:45–9:19			
A3/B3	Grade 9 teal orchestra	9:22–10:07			
A4	Grade 8 bass	10:10–10:55			
B4	Grade 8 cello	10:10–10:55			
A5	Prep	10:58–12:08			
A6/B6	Grade 9 black orchestra	12:11–12:56			
A7	Grade 8 violin	12:59–1:44			
B7	Grade 8 viola	12:59–1:44			
A8	Grade 8 violin	1:47–2:32			
B8	Grade 8 violin	1:47–2:32			
A9/B9	Prep	2:35–3:22			

Figure 11.

General Music Lesson Plan Page

Monday	Date			
Section	**Time**	**Prepare/present**	**Practice**	**Activity/Assess**
4–3	8:35			
4–4	9:00			
5–2	9:25			
5–3	9:50			
5–4	10:15			
Prep	**10:40**			
3–1	11:05			
3–3	11:30			
Lunch	**11:55**			
2–1	12:20			
2–2	12:45			
2–3	1:10			
Prep	**1:35**			
1–1				
1–4	2:25			

Chapter 7

Assessments

WHY IS IT IMPORTANT TO ASSESS?

Teachers need to know what students have learned, whether it be knowledge, skill, or process. Teachers also need to evaluate student understanding. Materials may have to be re-taught, or more practice may be needed on a particular concept. In other words, what do students know, how do we know what they have learned, and what are we going to do if they haven't learned it?

HOW DOES ASSESSMENT BENEFIT THE STUDENT?

When a teacher presents the expectations of an assessment before the assessment, students know exactly what to do for a particular grade. Offer feedback on what was done well and what needs improvement each time students are given an assessment and they will become more engaged learners and try harder to do their best independently. It is evident that all students want to participate and contribute to a class when the teacher has timely and frequent feedback on the progress toward learning targets. Allow students to redo assessments if they choose. This gives them a chance to improve. Always take the student's best score for a grade.

FORMATIVE AND SUMMATIVE ASSESSMENT

Formative assessment is assessment *for* learning which defines student progress toward the learning target and gives the teacher feedback on what is understood and what should be re-taught. By offering students feedback throughout learning and practicing concepts, they know exactly what their progress is toward mastery of skills and concepts. The information tells the teacher and student about the progress toward the learning target and is executed during learning.

Summative assessment is assessment *of* learning which defines student achievement or mastery of standards at a point in time. An example of this would be standardized tests, end-of-unit tests, or performance assessments after concerts. This information tells others how a student is doing and is executed after learning.

VARIETIES OF ASSESSMENTS

There are three kinds of assessment:

A. Diagnostic: indicates what a student needs to learn (pre-test)
B. Formative: indicates how a student is progressing throughout the learning process (short, quick assessments along the learning path)
C. Summative: indicates how a student did at the end of an activity or unit (final test or performance)

Items that should be assessed:

A. Basic knowledge and skills
B. Complex processes in student work
C. Student work through the learning process
D. Student's own feeling about work done
E. Student work at the end of a unit (remember, they should redo work if needed)

Both students and teachers can be involved in writing assessments, and both should be involved in assessing. Students may evaluate themselves or peer work. Once students assess their own or others' work, they view learning differently and take ownership of their own work. It becomes clear what a student needs to do to succeed. Assessments should not be work done for a grade, but the best work done by the student, resulting in feeling a sense of accomplishment and improvement.

Adults can easily remember taking a test, getting a grade, and never knowing what was wrong or having the opportunity to correct it. Today, students know the expectations, receive valuable feedback from others, and correct learning errors to reach mastery of a skill or concept.

There are many assessment tools to be used in the music classroom:

1. Checklist: a list of performance criteria
2. Rubrics: scoring guides
3. Questioning: asking questions periodically during learning
4. Paper and pencil test: multiple-choice, fill-in-the-blank, etc.
5. Self-assessment
6. Writing projects
7. Day-to-day observations
8. Culminating project or performance
9. Portfolio
10. Multimedia projects

CREATING ASSESSMENTS

Checklist

A checklist is a simple assessment that lists expectations. If students have a checklist prior to an assessment, they know exactly what expected and what will be assessed. On the checklist you can mark either what is done correctly or what needs attention. Marking what needs attention is quicker, and over time, it becomes evident what is not being corrected. If you use this procedure, make sure students understand that everything not marked is done as required and that it is the marked areas which need attention. If a few areas are repeatedly marked, it is evident that the student is not making necessary changes. This is a good feedback tool for students at the time of assessment and for parents at conferences. Performance assessments provide an opportunity to do a mini-less with the student to reinforce what is correct and what needs improvement.

Standard 2: Checklist Examples for Learning How to Hold a Clarinet, Flute, and Stringed Instrument

Figure 12.

Grade 6 Clarinet Position Checklist

Name

Assembly/Identifying Parts	Date	Date	Date	Date	Date	Date	Date
Write parts not identified in column: mouthpiece, ligature, reed, barrel, upper joint, lower joint , bell							
Grease all corks as needed.							
Using a twisting motion, connect the bell, lower joint, upper joint and barrel without applying pressure on the rods or damaging the bridge key mechanism.							
Place the ligature over the mouthpiece, followed by the moistened reed, heel first, down between the ligature and mouthpiece. Correctly align the reed and ligature.							
Maintenance/Care							
Condensation in the clarinet must be removed immediately after each use. Before cleaning, remove the mouthpiece, reed and ligature and store the reed appropriately. Wipe out the mouthpiece and the remaining parts using an absorbent cloth swab.							
Right Hand							
Form a relaxed curvature of the fingers with the finger pads poised above appropriate tone holes. Palm of hand near base of fingers should not make contact with the clarinet.							
Thumb under thumb rest near the thumb nail.							
Place pinky above right pinky cluster keys.							
Left Hand							
Form a relaxed curvature of the fingers with the finger pads poised above appropriate tone holes. Palm of hand near base of fingers should not make contact with the clarinet.							
Place thumb in a two o'clock position on or near the thumb tone hole.							
Place pinky above left pinky cluster keys.							

Figure 12. (continued)
Grade 6 Clarinet Position Checklist

Assembly/Identifying Parts	Date	Date	Date	Date	Date	Date	Date
Playing Position							
Sit on the edge of your chair, feet flat on the floor, and shoulders back.							
Looking straight ahead, bring the instrument to your mouth.							
With your elbows slightly away from your body, position the bell at your knees.							
Embouchure							
Firm the corners of your mouth.							
Flatten chin.							
Rest upper teeth on the top of the mouthpiece.							
Form lower lip as a cushion on bottom teeth.							
Seal the lips around the mouthpiece.							
Produce a sustained F# on the mouthpiece and barrel.							
Articulation Technique							
Release each air stream with the tip of the tongue touching the tip of the reed in an up and down motion.							
To produce groups of articulated notes, the tip of the tongue touches the tip of the reed over a continuous air stream.							
To produce groups of slurred notes, the tip of the tongue touches the tip of the reed only at the beginning of the curved line. The air stream remains steady as the notes and fingerings change.							

Note: Individual physical characteristics will affect and angle and alignment of the instrument.

Figure 13.

Grade 6 Flute Position Checklist

NAME

Assembly/Identifying Parts	Date	Date	Date	Date	Date	Date	Date
Write parts not identified in column: head, foot, and middle joints, embouchure hole, and tuning/cleaning rod.							
Assemble the three main pieces using continuous clockwise motion until in place.							
The rod of the foot joint is centered with tone holes and embouchure hole.							
Maintenance/Care							
Condensation in the flute must be removed immediately after each use, using an absorbent cloth attached to the cleaning rod. All cloths should be stored outside of the case with the exception of a silk cloth. Cleaning rod is kept inside the case.							
Right Hand							
Form a relaxed curvature of the fingers with finger pads in contact with keys.							
Thumb slightly curved underneath first and second fingers in a "C" shape.							
Pinky rests on the E-flat key.							
No bend in wrist.							
Left Hand							
The flute rests in the crook of the index finger.							
Form a relaxed curvature of the fingers with finger pads in contact with keys.							
Thumb in contact with one of the two thumb keys.							
Pinky rests on the A-flat key.							
Playing Position							
Sit on the edge of the chair, feet flat on the floor, and shoulders back.							
The instrument follows a loose horizontal line from the lip.							
Embouchure							
Embouchure hole on the head joint is parallel with the ceiling.							
Embouchure plate makes contact with the bottom lip.							
Blow relaxed lips apart with a gentle "pooh" sound.							
A triangle of condensation will form on the embouchure plate opposite the lips.							
Produce two to four tones on the head joint alone.							
Articulation Technique							
Release each air stream with the tip of the tongue touching the upper back of the top teeth.							
To produce groups of articulated notes, the tip of the tongue touches the upper back of the top teeth over a continuous air stream.							
To produce groups of slurred notes, the tip of the tongue touches the upper back of the top teeth only at the beginning of the curved line. The air stream remains steady as notes and fingerings change.							

Note: Individual physical characteristics will affect and angle and alignment of the instrument.

Figure 14.

Stringed Instrument Posture and Position

Checklist for Middle and High School

Name_____ School Year _____

Criteria will be checked only if attention is needed.

CRITERIA	DATE	DATE	DATE	DATE	DATE
Left Hand for Violin and Viola					
Wrist is vertically straight.					
Play on fingertips with rounded fingers.					
Elbow is under the instrument.					
Thumb is relaxed and across from the index finger.					
Left Hand and Arm for Cello and Bass					
Wrist and forearm are aligned.					
Play on fingertips with rounded fingers.					
Thumb is relaxed and behind the second finger.					
Arm is away from the body and at the appropriate height for string(s) played.					
Bow Hold for Violin, Viola, Cello, and Bass French Bow					
Fingers are rounded and relaxed.					
Thumb knuckle is curved out.					
Violin and viola: place pinky on top of the frog.					
Cello and French bass bow: second finger is aligned with the metal (ferrule).					
Cello and French bass bow: pinkies are over the frog. (Pinky placement is the teacher's choice for cello.)					
Student pronates to the left for tone production.					
German bass bow: proper finger placement					
Fingers are rounded and relaxed.					
First finger touches frog and fourth finger touches metal ferrule.					
Second and third fingers are curved inside opening of frog.					
Bow Technique					
Use proper bow placement(s).					
Use proper bow speed(s).					
Use proper bow weight(s).					
Moves the bow in a straight path.					
Violin and viola: bow from the elbow down.					
Cello and French Bass bow: sink whole arm weight into the string.					
German bass bow: rotate hand and arm to the left for tone.					
Posture					
Instrument is placed correctly.					
Sit on the front edge of chair or stool with back straight and feet on the floor.					
Stand with correct posture.					

Checklist Example for Elementary Recorder Skills
This simple assessment allows a list of criteria to be evaluated by the student and then the teacher. It requires checking one of two choices—skill achieved or in progress. This checklist makes the student aware of the aspects of playing recorder and progress toward mastery of these concepts.

Figure 15.
Elementary Recorder Skills Assessment

Name _____

Recorder Skills Assessment

Notes: B–A–G

Write the date you are "in progress" and the date the skill is achieved.

1. **Hand position**
   Left hand on top; right hand below.

   Student _____ skill achieved _____ in progress
   Teacher _____ skill achieved _____ in progress

2. **Tonguing**
   Tongue goes to the roof of the mouth, producing the sound "doo" with a steady air stream.

   Student _____ skill achieved _____ in progress
   Teacher _____ skill achieved _____ in progress

3. **Tone Quality**
   Mouth is sealed around the mouthpiece with "warm" air flowing.

   Student _____ skill achieved _____ in progress
   Teacher _____ skill achieved _____ in progress

4. **Melody**
   Demonstrate proper fingerings for the chosen song.

   Student _____ skill achieved _____ in progress
   Teacher _____ skill achieved _____ in progress

This is what I think I do best on recorder

_____

_____

_____

This is what I need to work on

_____

_____

_____

RUBRICS

A rubric is a scoring tool that lists the criteria or learning targets to be assessed down the left side and graduated qualitative statements of accomplishment to the right of each criterion.

Most rubrics are based on four statements or levels of accomplishment:

4. Activity was executed with exceptional ease or creativity (advanced)
3. Grade-level expectation; mastery of skill or concept (proficient)
2. Understanding and working on a skill or concept but has not mastered it (partially proficient)
1. Beginning stages of working toward a learning target (novice)

Most students should be at level 3, a few at levels 4 and 2 and in rare circumstances a couple of students at level 1.

Levels 1 and 2 should not be used as negative feedback. Instead, show students how much growth has occurred and how they are on their way to mastering a concept or skill. Provide them with feedback on what is going well and what is needed to accomplish mastery. When writing levels 2 and 1, make sure statements are written in a positive, encouraging manner.

When Writing Rubrics

1. Write level 3 first (what would you expect at this grade level). Go to level 4 next, then level 2 and level 1 last.
2. Each rubric criterion should focus on a single concept or skill. Combining several items to evaluate in one section makes assessment confusing.
3. Write the most- to least-important criteria from the top to bottom of the rubric.
4. Write positive statements that encourage lower-level students to work toward mastery.
5. Avoid writing criteria that count mistakes.
6. Avoid subjective words such as good, acceptable, or poor.
7. Try to use a common sentence stem that can be added to for varying levels.
8. Number the criteria to make them easy to select and to notify students which will be assessed.

Benefits of Using Rubrics

1. Rubrics reduce the time teachers spend assessing because students already know expectations and are able to do well the first time.
2. Parents like rubrics because they aid in helping with homework more intelligently.
3. Students are more responsible for their work.
4. Writing a general rubric, such as vocal performance, is efficient. It can be used on anything performed vocally, whether an exercise, warm-up, or literature excerpt.

EXAMPLES OF RUBRICS

Standard 1: Choral Performance Rubric

The Choral Assessment Rubric is designed to list all of the learning targets of a vocal performance. In this figure 16 there are twelve numbered criteria or targets. For some assessments, only targets 1, 2, 3 and 4 may be selected. On other assessments, a particular target may be the only item to assess, such as diction if learning a song in a foreign language.

Since some targets may be more important than others, consider assigning weight values to calculate scores for letter grades are needed (see figure 16).

Figure 16.

Assigning Weight Values for Score Calculation

Category	Points	Level	Subtotal
Tone	20	3	60
Accuracy	20	2	40
Diction	10	3	30
Total points received on this assessment			130
Total points for assessment (50 at Level 3)			150

Students received 87% on this assessment.

Note

Some grading programs allow maximum points allowed. The key word is "allowed" as opposed to total points on the assessment. To figure the total points, take fifty points times level three (proficiency or mastery) which equals 150 points. The total points *allowed* is fifty points times level 4 (advanced) which equals 200 points.

Figure 17.

High School Vocal Performance Assessment

(Live or Recorded)

Name _____   Piece _____

		LEVEL 4	LEVEL 3	LEVEL 2	LEVEL 1
1	Tone Quality	Sings expressively, using appropriate, consistent tone quality for selection.	Uses appropriate, consistent tone quality for selection.	Generally uses appropriate, consistent tone quality for selection.	Is beginning to develop appropriate tone quality for selection.
2	Notes	Sings all notes with precision and fluency in proper, steady tempo.	Sings all notes accurately in steady tempo.	Sings most notes accurately, varying tempo when necessary to accommodate unfamiliar sections.	Sings some notes accurately, varying tempo when necessary to accommodate unfamiliar sections.
3	Intonation	Sings all notes in center of pitch with precision and fluency.	Sings notes in center of pitch, correcting notes when incorrect.	Sings several notes sharp or flat.	Sings most notes sharp or flat.
4	Phrasing/Breath	Uses breath management to support sensitive and expressive phrasing.	Uses breath management to support appropriate phrasing.	Generally uses breath management to support appropriate phrasing.	Is beginning to learn breath management to support appropriate phrasing.
5	Rhythmic Accuracy	Sings all rhythms with precision and fluency in proper, steady tempo.	Sings all rhythms accurately in steady tempo.	Sings most rhythms accurately, varying tempo when necessary to accommodate unfamiliar sections.	Sings some rhythms accurately, varying tempo when necessary to accommodate unfamiliar sections.
6	Diction	Sings all words in a distinguishable manner for selection, demonstrating appropriate vocal diction to sing expressively.	Sings all words in a distinguishable manner for selection.	Sings most words in a distinguishable manner for selection.	Sings some words in a distinguishable manner for selection.
7	Vowel Placement	Sings all tall, open, distinguishable vowels appropriate for good choral singing, demonstrating expressive vocal techniques.	Sings all tall, open, distinguishable vowels appropriate for good choral singing.	Sings mostly tall, open, distinguishable vowels appropriate for good choral singing.	Sings some tall, open, distinguishable vowels appropriate for good choral singing.
8	Dynamic Levels	Performs dynamics at appropriate levels in a distinct and sensitive manner.	Performs dynamics at appropriate levels.	Performs most dynamics at appropriate levels.	Performs some dynamics at appropriate level.
9	Interpretation	Instinctively demonstrates appropriate interpretation of piece through facial expression, physical sensitivity, and verbalizing textual meaning.	Demonstrates appropriate interpretation of piece through facial expression, physical sensitivity, and verbalizing textual meaning.	Generally demonstrates appropriate interpretation of piece through facial expression, physical sensitivity, and verbalizing textual meaning.	Is beginning to demonstrate appropriate interpretation of piece through facial expression, physical sensitivity, and verbalizing textual meaning.
10	Ensemble Precision	Performs precise entrances and cut-offs appropriate to selection.	Performs entrances and cut-offs appropriate to selection.	Performs some entrances and cut-offs appropriate to selection.	Performs a few entrances and cut-offs appropriate to selection.
11	Balance	Sings with a sensitive awareness of appropriate balance.	Sings with an awareness of appropriate balance.	Generally sings with awareness of appropriate balance.	Is beginning to sing with awareness of appropriate balance.
12	Blend	Sings with a sensitive awareness of appropriate blend.	Sings with an awareness of appropriate blend.	Generally sings with awareness of appropriate blend.	Is beginning to sing with awareness of appropriate blend.

Students may assess each other by having a copy of the rubrics and using the Quick Assessment form.

1. Students place their own name under *Name of Evaluator.*

2. Place the name of the performer or performing group under *Name of Performance.*

3. Use rubric statements to evaluate the performance.

4. Under comments, write one positive aspect about the performance and something performers could work on to improve the performance.

5. This can now be used two ways.

   a. Evaluate the student's assessment of the performance for a grade.

   b. Cut off the *Name of Evaluator* at the top of the form and give the remainder of the form to the performers for feedback. When students evaluate others, they are more critical about their own practice and performance.

Figure 18.
Choral Quick Assessment

Name of Evaluator				
Name of Performance				
Tone Quality	4	3	2	1
Notes	4	3	2	1
Intonation	4	3	2	1
Phrase/Breath	4	3	2	1
Rhythm	4	3	2	1
Diction	4	3	2	1
Vowel Placement	4	3	2	1
Dynamics	4	3	2	1
Interpretation	4	3	2	1
Ensemble	4	3	2	1
Balance	4	3	2	1
Blend	4	3	2	1
Comments: (1 positive and 1 improvement)				

Name of Evaluator				
Name of Performance				
Tone Quality	4	3	2	1
Notes	4	3	2	1
Intonation	4	3	2	1
Phrase/Breath	4	3	2	1
Rhythm	4	3	2	1
Diction	4	3	2	1
Vowel Placement	4	3	2	1
Dynamics	4	3	2	1
Interpretation	4	3	2	1
Ensemble	4	3	2	1
Balance	4	3	2	1
Blend	4	3	2	1
Comments: (1 positive and 1 improvement)				

Name of Evaluator				
Name of Performance				
Tone Quality	4	3	2	1
Notes	4	3	2	1
Intonation	4	3	2	1
Phrase/Breath	4	3	2	1
Rhythm	4	3	2	1
Diction	4	3	2	1
Vowel Placement	4	3	2	1
Dynamics	4	3	2	1
Interpretation	4	3	2	1
Ensemble	4	3	2	1
Balance	4	3	2	1
Blend	4	3	2	1
Comments: (1 positive and 1 improvement)				

Name of Evaluator				
Name of Performance				
Tone Quality	4	3	2	1
Notes	4	3	2	1
Intonation	4	3	2	1
Phrase/Breath	4	3	2	1
Rhythm	4	3	2	1
Diction	4	3	2	1
Vowel Placement	4	3	2	1
Dynamics	4	3	2	1
Interpretation	4	3	2	1
Ensemble	4	3	2	1
Balance	4	3	2	1
Blend	4	3	2	1
Comments: (1 positive and 1 improvement)				

A kid-friendly choral assessment for elementary students may look like the one in figure 19.

Figure 19.
Elementary Vocal Performance Assessment

Name _____   Piece _____

		LEVEL 4	LEVEL 3	LEVEL 2	LEVEL 1
1	Notes	Sings all notes in tune.	Sings most notes in tune.	Sings lower notes in tune and is working on upper range.	Sings some notes in a singing voice and others with a speaking voice.
2	Rhythmic Accuracy	Sings all rhythms correctly with a steady beat.	Sings most rhythms correctly with a steady beat.	Sings most rhythms correctly and changes speed of the beat when difficult.	Is beginning to sing rhythms correctly.
3	Vowel and Consonant Pronunciation	Sings with tall vowels and clear consonants for every word to be understood.	Sings most words with tall vowels and clear consonants and text is understood.	Is developing tall vowels and clear consonants for understanding of the text.	Is beginning to sing tall vowels and clear consonants for understanding of text.
4	Tone and Breath Support	Uses enough air to produce a clear tone, especially in upper notes.	Uses enough air to produce a clear tone for lower notes and some upper notes.	Uses enough air only for lower notes.	Is developing air support.
5	Singing Together (Ensemble)	Makes precise entrances and cutoffs and stays together the entire song.	Enters, cuts off, and stays together the entire song.	Is developing entrances, cutoffs, and staying together during the song.	Is beginning to enter, cutoff, and stay together in parts of song.

Standard 2: Instrumental Performance Assessment for High School

It is best to write the high school rubric first and then take from this to create middle and elementary school rubrics. Wording and criteria may be adjusted for age level.

Figure 20.
Secondary Strings Performance Assessment

Name _____   Piece _____

	LEVEL 4	LEVEL 3	LEVEL 2	LEVEL 1
1 Tone Quality	Uses proper bow placement, speed, and weight appropriate for musical selection and demonstrates advanced bow techniques to play expressively.	Uses proper bow placement, speed and weight appropriate for musical selection.	Generally uses proper bow placement, speed, and weight.	Begins to understand bow placement, speed, and weight.
2 Notes	Plays all notes with precision and fluency in a proper steady tempo.	Plays all notes accurately in a steady tempo.	Plays most notes accurately, varying tempo when necessary to accommodate unfamiliar sections.	Plays some notes accurately, varying tempo when necessary to accommodate unfamiliar sections.
3 Intonation	Plays all notes in center of pitch.	Plays notes in center of pitch, correcting pitches that are incorrect.	Plays several notes sharp or flat, affected by hand placement or lack of key signature knowledge.	Plays most notes sharp or flat, affected by hand placement or lack of key signature knowledge.
4 Rhythmic Accuracy	Plays all rhythms with precision and fluency in a proper steady tempo.	Plays all rhythms accurately in a steady tempo.	Plays most rhythms accurately, varying tempo when necessary to accommodate unfamiliar sections.	Plays some rhythms accurately, varying tempo when necessary to accommodate unfamiliar sections.
5 Articulation	Plays all articulations correctly, making smooth transitions from one to another in a musical manner.	Plays all articulations correctly.	Plays most articulations correctly.	Plays some articulations correctly.
Dynamic Levels	Performs dynamics at the appropriate levels in a distinct and sensitive manner.	Performs dynamics at appropriate levels with noticeable contrast.	Performs appropriate dynamics and begins to increase contrast in dynamic levels.	Begins to develop ability to control dynamic levels.
Positions	Shifts from one note to another in a relaxed, fluid manner using creative fingerings to accommodate passages.	Shifts from one note to another accurately with a relaxed, fluid motion.	Shifts from one note to another with a somewhat fluid motion and accuracy level.	Understands concept of shifting and is working toward accuracy and fluidity.
Vibrato	Plays with a consistent, relaxed vibrato, changing speeds to produce musical effects.	Plays with a consistent, relaxed vibrato.	Is developing vibrato skills and is working on a consistent and relaxed motion.	Is adding beginning stages of vibrato to longer notes.
Ensemble Precision	Performs precise entrances and cutoffs appropriate to selection.	Performs entrances and cutoffs appropriate to selection.	Performs some entrances and cutoffs appropriate to selection.	Performs some entrances and cutoffs appropriate to selection.
Balance	Plays with a sensitive awareness of balance.	Plays with awareness of appropriate balance.	Generally plays with awareness of appropriate balance.	Is beginning to play with awareness of appropriate balance.

Figure 21.

Secondary Wind Performance Assessment

Name _____   Piece _____

		LEVEL 4	LEVEL 3	LEVEL 2	LEVEL 1
1	Tone Breath Support	Plays with mature characteristic sound appropriate to instrument using proper breathing techniques.	Plays with a characteristic sound appropriate to instrument using proper breathing techniques.	Is developing a characteristic sound appropriate for instrument along with proper breathing techniques.	Understands basic principles of tone production and breathing techniques.
2	Intonation	Demonstrates precise intonation and readily adjusts to pitch discrepancies.	Understands intonation tendencies and adjusts to pitch discrepancies.	Recognizes pitch discrepancies and begins to make adjustments.	Begins to recognize pitch discrepancies.
3	Notes	Plays notes with precision and fluency in a proper steady tempo.	Plays notes accurately in a steady tempo.	Plays most notes accurately, varying tempo when necessary to accommodate unfamiliar sections.	Plays some notes accurately, varying tempo when necessary to accommodate unfamiliar sections.
4	Rhythm	Plays rhythms, including complex rhythms, with correct division of beat precisely and fluently in a proper steady tempo.	Plays rhythms with correct division of beat in a steady tempo.	Plays most rhythms accurately, varying tempo when necessary to accommodate unfamiliar sections.	Plays some rhythms accurately, playing simple divisions of beat correctly and varying tempo when necessary to accommodate unfamiliar sections.
5	Articulation	Plays all articulations correctly, making smooth transitions from one to another in a musical manner.	Plays all articulations correctly.	Plays most articulations correctly.	Plays some articulations correctly.
6	Dynamics	Performs dynamics at appropriate levels distinctly and sensitively throughout range of instrument.	Performs dynamics at appropriate levels with noticeable contrast.	Performs most appropriate dynamics with minimal contrast in dynamic levels.	Begins to develop ability to control dynamic levels.
7	Ensemble	Is instinctively sensitive to balance, phrasing, articulation, and dynamics, and communicates nonverbal cues well.	Is sensitive to balance, phrasing, articulation, and dynamics, and communicates nonverbal cues often.	Is somewhat sensitive to balance, phrasing, articulation, and dynamics, and is beginning to communicate nonverbal cues.	Is becoming sensitive to balance, phrasing, articulation, dynamics, and cuing.

Standard 3: Improvisation and Standard 4: Composition Rubrics

Improvisation and composition rubrics may be the same for elementary general music, band, choir, and orchestra. Determine what is appropriate for elementary, middle, and high school levels.

Figure 22.

Middle and High School Improvisation Assessment

Name _____   Piece _____

		LEVEL 4	LEVEL 3	LEVEL 2	LEVEL 1
1	Melody	Uses required notes accurately and creatively.	Uses required notes accurately.	Generally uses required notes accurately.	Is developing accurate use of required notes.
2	Rhythm	Uses required rhythms accurately and creatively.	Uses required rhythms accurately.	Generally uses required rhythms accurately.	Is developing accurate use of required rhythms.
3	Tempo	Creatively varies tempo to increase appeal.	Performs in a steady tempo.	Generally performs in a steady tempo.	Is developing a steady tempo.
4	Phrasing	Instinctively and creatively uses phrasing to add interest to the improvisation and creates a clear ending.	Uses distinguishable phrasing and creates a clear ending.	Is developing phrasing and a clear ending.	Is beginning to feel the number of beats in a phrase and to understand how to create a clear ending.
5	Dynamics	Instinctively and creatively uses dynamics to add interest to the improvisation.	Uses distinguishable dynamics.	Is developing dynamic use.	Is beginning to use dynamics.

Figure 23.

Middle and High School Composition Assessment

Name _____ **Grading Period 1 2 3 4**

CRITERIA	LEVEL 4	LEVEL 3	LEVEL 2	LEVEL 1	LEVEL ATTAINED
Neatness	Extremely clear and readable by others.	Clear and readable by others.	Generally readable by others but unclear in spots.	Willing to rewrite so composition is readable by others.	
Rhythmic Accuracy	High understanding of counting system. Shows creativity and variety with rhythm.	Uses appropriate number of beats per measure.	Generally uses appropriate number of beats per measure.	Beginning to understand appropriate number of beats per measure.	
Melodic Accuracy	Shows imagination using notes within specific guidelines.	Uses notes within specified guidelines.	Generally uses notes within specified guidelines.	Beginning stages of using notes within specified guidelines.	
Harmonic Accuracy	Shows imagination using harmonies within specific guidelines.	Uses harmonies within specified guidelines.	Generally uses harmonies within specified guidelines.	Beginning stages of using harmonies within specified guidelines.	
Articulations and Musical Markings	Shows imagination with articulations and musical markings.	Uses articulations and musical markings appropriately.	Generally uses articulations and musical markings appropriately.	Beginning stages of using articulations and musical markings appropriately.	

Standard 5: Rhythm Rubric

There are three aspects of rhythm: counting, playing or singing, and labeling. Rhythm rubrics are written so that these learning targets can be kept separate.

Figure 24.

Middle and High School Rhythm Rubric

Name _____ Grading Period 1 2 3 4

CRITERIA	LEVEL 4	LEVEL 3	LEVEL 2	LEVEL 1	LEVEL ATTAINED
Count and Clap Rhythms	Responds correctly on all rhythms with ease and precision.	Responds correctly on all rhythms.	Responds correctly on most rhythms.	Responds correctly on some rhythms.	
Playing Rhythms	Responds correctly on all rhythms with ease and precision.	Responds correctly on all rhythms.	Responds correctly on most rhythms.	Responds correctly on some rhythms.	
Labeling Rhythms	Responds correctly on all rhythms with ease and precision.	Responds correctly on all rhythms.	Responds correctly on most rhythms.	Responds correctly on some rhythms.	

Standards 6 and 7: Listening and Evaluating Music Using Six Traits Writing Rubric

Several districts require Six Traits writing skills and assessment. When students write reactions to music or performances, this rubric may be used to evaluate student writing.

Figure 25.

Six Traits of Writing Rubric

Name _____

	LEVEL 4	LEVEL 3	LEVEL 2	LEVEL 1
Ideas	Ideas have rich details that draw reader in.	Ideas are clear, informative, and interesting.	Ideas are emerging and developing.	Ideas are developing with assistance.
Organization	Organization allows recognizable sequencing from a strong beginning to a sense of resolution.	Organization allows easy transition from topic to topic.	Some organization emerging and developing.	Beginning, simple stages of organization.
Voice	Has a strong sense of how to convey message to reader.	Displays engagement with reader at various times.	Some sense of commitment to topic is evident.	Limited commitment to topic is evident.
Word Choice	Rich, robust words used to energize writing.	Word choice is interesting and used properly.	Some interesting use of word choice.	Limited vocabulary is evident.
Sentence Fluency	Writing has rhythm, moving effortlessly from sentence to sentence.	Simple and complex sentences are fluent and easy to understand.	Good simple sentence structure along with developing complex sentence structure.	Good simple sentence structure.
Conventions	Uses a wide range of conventions with little or no need to edit.	Uses correct conventions.	Some correct conventions used.	Limited correct conventions used.

Self Evaluation

Students should self-evaluate frequently. Any rubric could be used for this. At the end of a grading period, students can assess their attitude toward material presented, learning, behavior, and preparation for class. The assessment in figure 26 is used for an instrumental large-group setting, but could be adapted for choral or other settings.

Figure 26.

Self Evaluation

NAME _____ Quarter 1 2 3 4

This quarterly self-evaluation will show your attitude toward learning, and your behavior and preparation for this class. It is an opportunity to show your strengths and to determine what areas you could continue to work on.

4 = always
3 = most of the time
2 = some of the time
1 = rarely

_____ 1. I have good attendance and am punctual to class.

_____ 2. I come to class with the attitude that I can make a contribution to this group.

_____ 3. I am well prepared for class and practice so that I know my part.

_____ 4. I work on my posture or playing position so that I may play to the best of my ability.

_____ 5. I am able to look around the notes at dynamics, articulation and style while I play.

_____ 6. I learn my music thoroughly so that I am able to watch the conductor while I play.

_____ 7. I do not talk or play my instrument during class unless I am asked to do so.

_____ 8. My folder is organized and I mark music carefully using only pencil.

_____ 9. I enjoy learning new music or music of different styles or cultures.

_____ 10. I appreciate seeing my teacher's evaluations and work on the areas that show that I need improvement.

What is one thing you are proud of this grading period?

_____

What is one thing you would like to improve for the next grading period?

_____

The elementary self-evaluation in figure 27 uses the three simple responses of yes, sometimes, or no. At the bottom of the form, students are given the opportunity to offer comments and set learning goals. The teacher also has an opportunity to respond to students' answers.

Figure 27.

Elementary Self-reflection of
Musical Work, Grades 4–5

Name _____

Class _____

Date _____

Yes	Sometimes	No	Skills
			1. When singing, I breathe deeply to produce a good tone.
			2. I pronounce my words carefully, paying attention to the beginning and ending sounds of words.
			3. I play with good mallet technique. I hold my mallets correctly, alternate mallets, and bounce gently.
			4. I can tell if a song is *Do*- or *La*-based (major or minor).
			5. I can perform an instrument part independently.
			6. I can play the notes B–A–G comfortably on the recorder.
			7. I can read all the notes on the treble clef staff.
			8. I always perform and listen with enthusiasm in music class.
			9. I am polite and respectful of others in music class.

Student comments (Comment on activities you enjoyed or didn't enjoy, something you learned this nine weeks, or something you can do better now than last nine weeks, etc.)

_____

_____

_____

Student goals for next nine weeks _____

_____

_____

Teacher comments_____

_____

_____

Standard 2: Tuning Assessment Rubric

It is important for instrumental music students to be able to tune their own instruments. With instruments, there is a process to tuning:

1. Hearing in- or out-of-tune pitches
2. Deciding whether the note played is higher, lower, or the same as the tuning pitch
3. Executing the tuning process with teacher assistance
4. Executing the tuning process independently

Figure 28.

Sequence of Tuning Procedure

Assessment for Timpani

Name _____

Date _____

		LEVEL 4	LEVEL 3	LEVEL 2	LEVEL 1
1	Knows the pitch range of each timpanum. Circle those that are known. 32" 29" 26" 23" D–A F–C B-flat–F D–A	Ease and understanding of procedure.	Understands and executes procedure.	Executes procedure with some assistance.	Executes procedure only with assistance.
2	Matches timpani pitch to given fixed pitch tuning from low to high.	Ease and understanding of procedure.	Understands and executes procedure.	Executes procedure with some assistance.	Executes procedure only with assistance.
3	Changes pitches within a piece.	Ease and understanding of procedure.	Understands and executes procedure.	Executes procedure with some assistance.	Executes procedure only with assistance.
4	Tunes in intervals M2 m2 M3 m3 P4 tritone P5 (A4, D5) M6 m6 M7 m7 P8 **Circle those assessed and check those that are correct.**	Ease and understanding of procedure.	Understands and executes procedure.	Executes procedure with some assistance.	Executes procedure only with assistance.

Figure 29.
Sequence of Tuning Procedure
Assessment for Strings

Name _____

Date _____

		LEVEL 4	LEVEL 3	LEVEL 2	LEVEL 1
1	Identifies in tune or out of tune. Circle those correctly identified. A D G C E	Ease and understanding of procedure.	Understands and executes procedure.	Executes procedure with some assistance.	Executes procedure only with assistance.
2	Identifies if pitch is lower, higher, or the same. Circle those correctly identified. A D G C E	Ease and understanding of procedure.	Understands and executes procedure.	Executes procedure with some assistance.	Executes procedure only with assistance.
3	Tunes with fine tuners. Circle those correctly executed. A D G C E	Ease and understanding of procedure.	Understands and executes procedure.	Executes procedure with some assistance.	Executes procedure only with assistance.
4	Tunes with peg. Circle those correctly executed. A D G C E	Ease and understanding of procedure.	Understands and executes procedure.	Executes procedure with some assistance.	Executes procedure only with assistance.

Students Involved in Writing Assessments

Teachers can draw learning targets (the learning goals in the leftmost column on a rubric) from the district curriculum and from students in a discussion. After teaching a topic or concept, stop and ask students to go through the steps of learning how to play an instrument or, in a performance, what aspects are expected for a good performance. Students actively involved in the decision-making or assessment-writing process will be more active participants in their own education.

Some questions to stimulate discussion among students and teachers writing a rubric together regarding a group musical performance:

1. What is required to execute clean entrances and cut-offs together?
2. What are the aspects of musicality in a performance?
3. What are the technical aspects of performance?
4. What do you need to know about symbols and terms in order to perform a piece correctly?
5. Why do students need to watch a conductor?

Chapter 8

Organizing Assessment Documentation

QUICK, NON-INTRUSIVE IN-CLASS ASSESSMENTS

There are many quick ways to assess a student without interrupting class time. While a student plays or sings a familiar and practiced measure, line, or exercise individually, the teacher can hear the student's progress on new concepts. All students should participate, whether all on the same day or over several days. This takes very little time.

If students are uncomfortable playing or singing in front of the class, make sure there is an option to perform for the teacher at another time until they feel comfortable performing for their peers. This is important to student comfort level and future performances.

Make sure students understand that it is okay to make a mistake. Never allow other students to make fun of someone if a mistake is made. Emphasize that your classroom is a place to learn, and mistakes are often made when practicing and even assessing a concept. Allow students another chance to improve if the first performance does not go well.

Students clapping and counting rhythms on a flash card or saying note names of a section of music also gives the teacher feedback on knowledge learned and takes very little time. Smaller samples of student work are all that is needed when assessing.

The next level of quick assessment is to transfer concepts learned by having students clap rhythms, say note names, or sightread unfamiliar material. When students attempt to transfer knowledge from known to unknown material, the teacher can check for understanding.

To document results quickly and easily in class, create a landscape-mode form with learning targets or tasks horizontally across the top and students' names vertically on the left.

To leave options open as to what to assess, create a simple form can to add daily assessments as they occur, similar to a grade book but standards-oriented. This also gives the teacher a quick glance at what areas need attention in both lesson material and assessment.

Figure 30.

Quarterly Fill-in Assessment

Quarterly Assessments (circle which quarter)   1   2   3   4

Class Period_____

Type of Assessment

Name of Student							

Information collected on these quick-assessment forms can easily be transferred to a grade book or individual assessment page which documents progress for each student.

There are several ways to quickly document assessments in a classroom setting. In instrumental classes, Standard 2 is assessed more frequently and in greater detail than others.

Figure 31 shows an assessment form that provides a way to document progress on all standards but Standard 2. The form in figure 32 is dedicated to the more specific aspects of Standard 2.

For a choral class, the form in figure 31 should include all standards but Standard 1, and the form in figure 32 should include only the learning targets for Standard 1.

Elementary teachers may assess singing and instrumental performance more than the other standards. In this case, three forms may prove useful: one that documents assessments for all standards but Standards 1 and 2, another for Standard 1 only, and a third for Standard 2 alone.

Figure 31.
Elementary Class Assessment (All but Standard 2)

Standards 1 3 4 5 6 7 8 9

Circle quarter   1   2   3   4

Class Period_____

4 = Does with ease or instinctively
3 = Grade level expectation
2 = Working on concept and progressing
1 = Beginning stages

	Sing	Improvise	Compose and Arrange	Read and Notate	Listen, Analyze, and Describe Music	Evaluate and Perform Music	Relate Other Music Arts Discovery	History and Culture
	1	3	4	5	6	7	8	9
Name of Student								

Figure 32.

Elementary Class Assessment Standard 2

Standard 2 Performance

Circle quarter   1   2   3   4

Class Period_____

4 = Does with ease or instinctively
3 = Grade level expectation
2 = Working on concept and progressing
1 = Beginning stages

	Tone	Notes	Intonation	Rhythm	Articulation	Dynamics	Posture Comments
Name of Student							

Elementary teachers struggle with recording assessment scores for hundreds of students.

Even though the curriculum is written by grade level and by standard, combinations of standards can be used for reporting to parents.

Figure 33.

General Music Report Card Grade 3

General Music Report Card Grade 3

4 = advanced   M = modified
3 = proficient   / = not assessed
2 = partially proficient
1 = novice

Music Performance		1	2	3
Standard 1	Sings independently on pitch.			
	Sings independently with correct rhythms.			
	Sings expressively.			
	Sings in parts.			
Standard 2	Performs independently with a steady beat.			
	Performs with proper posture and playing technique.			
	Performs in parts.			
Creates Music				
Standard 3	Improvises			
Standard 4	Composes			
Read and Write Music				
Standard 5	Rhythms			
	Notation			
	Symbols			
	Terms			
Listens to Music - Analyzes and Evaluates Music				
Standards 6 and 7	Describes with correct terminology.			
	Recognizes musical form.			
	Respect for others' performances and opinions.			
Culture & History				
Standards 8 and 9	Understands relationship of music to other subjects, culture, and history.			

The grade book can reflect combinations of standards. Instead of using a preprinted grade book, make copies of the form in figure 34 and enter student names in the leftmost column. Each class section should have a page for each quarter.

Each section provides three opportunities to assess and enter scores. In your spreadsheet program, apply a formula to the column labeled A (for "average") that averages the scores in columns 1–3. This number can be entered into grading software (or by hand if you do not use grading software).

You may want to consider looking at scores as students progress over the grading period. You would not average the grade, but use growth over time for the grade instead. If students improve from rubric level 2 to rubric level 3, they should have level 3 posted on the report card.

Space to write assessments given is at the bottom of the form. Keep in mind the score entered will be a rubric number taken from the rubric scoring guides created for each assessment.

Figure 34.
Elementary Grade Book

	Vocal				Instrumental				Create				Read / Write				Listen/Analyze				History/Culture			
Name	1	2	3	A	1	2	3	A	1	2	3	A	1	2	3	A	1	2	3	A	1	2	3	A

Write assessment name here

A = Average

Circle Quarter 1 2 3

DOCUMENTATION

It is sometimes useful to have a separate grading page for each student so that other students' grades are not seen when sharing assessment information. The Individual Student Assessment form in figure 35 is a handy tool for evaluating students quarterly. This assessment has a variety of learning targets that address standards and is a nice tool to include in an end-of-year portfolio. Notice the quarter can be circled at the top of the page to identify the grading period. As with other forms, the score entered is based on rubrics written for each particular assessment.

Figure 35.

Individual High School Student Assessment, Grades 9–12

Individual Instrumental Assessment Page Grades 9-12

Name_____

Rating Scale   4 = Exceptional
                            3 = At the appropriate Level
                            2 = Making progress
                            1 = Beginning stages

	Evaluation 1	Evaluation 2	Evaluation 3	Evaluation 4
Singing Standard 1				
Playing Standard 2	Tone	Tone	Tone	Tone
	Intonation	Intonation	Intonation	Intonation
	Rhythm	Rhythm	Rhythm	Rhythm
	Articulation	Articulation	Articulation	Articulation
	Dynamics	Dynamics	Dynamics	Dynamics
	Position	Position	Position	Position
	Vibrato	Vibrato	Vibrato	Vibrato
Playing scales · Standard 2				
Improvisation · Standard 3				
Composition and arranging · Standard 4				
Transposition · Standard 4				
Writing scales · Standard 5				
Counting rhythms · Standard 5				
Rhythmic dictation · Standard 5				
Melodic dictation · Standard 5				
Rhythmic and melodic dictation · Standard 5				
Listening · Standard 6				
Evaluation of self and others · Standard 7				
Music and other disciplines · Standard 8				
Music and history and culture · Standard 9				
Tuning · Standard 10				

Another way to record individual progress is to create a list of benchmarks that should be reported to students and parents (see figure 36). These are excellent for feedback at parent/teacher conferences or as progress reports, and can be put into student portfolios. Complete a progress report for each student and make a reference copy before sending it home at the end of the quarter or giving it to parents at conferences. This can also be placed in a portfolio.

This form includes standards, specific benchmarks to assess, ratings, and comments, and is a compact way to report work done toward meeting the standards. Remember, not all benchmarks have to be assessed. The teacher or a group of teachers can decide what is important to assess on the form. On this particular form, school district strategic plan goals, such as academic performance, character and life skills are listed and applied to music skills. This demonstrates to the district that music teachers are aware of the strategic plan and incorporate the elements into instruction.

Figure 36.

Standards-based Progress Report for Grade 6 Orchestra

Grade 6 Orchestra Progress Report

Name _____

Year _____

Rating Scale   4 = Exceeds expectations
3 = Expected at this grade level
2 = Working on this concept and progressing
1 = Beginning stages of development

Standard			Concept	Rating	Comments
1	**Singing**	1.8.1	Sings with accurate pitches and rhythms		
2	**Performance**	2.8.1	One octave scale		
		2.8.1	Correct posture and bow hold		
		2.8.1	Performs a variety of articulations		
		2.8.2	Performs expressively		
		2.8.3	Performs in an orchestra		
3	**Improvisation**	3.8.2	Improvises rhythmic variations		
		3.8.3	Improvises short melodies, given a set of notes and rhythms		
4	**Composition**	4.8.1	Composes simple ABA piece		
		4.8.2	Arranges accompaniment for melody with tonic and dominant chords		
5	**Reading music**	5.8.1	Labels rhythms		
		5.8.1	Labels notes		
		5.8.2	Sightreads simple melodies		
		5.8.3	Knows articulation notation		
		5.8.3	Knows dynamics notation		
6	**Listening**	6.8.1	Knows appropriate terminology to describe musical selections		
7	**Evaluating music**	7.8.1	Self-evaluation		
		7.8.2	Evaluates others positively		
8	**Music and other subjects**	8.8.1	Understands how emotions are portrayed in drama, visual art, and dance		
9	**History and culture**	9.8.1	Knows characteristics of a variety of music cultures		
		9.8.4	Proper audience behavior		
10	**Care of instrument**	10.8.1	Care of instrument and bow		
		10.8.2	Tunes with guidance		

Fargo Public Schools Strategic Plan Goals				Rating	Comment
Academic performance: lessons well prepared					
Character - Cooperation and Attitude					
Life Skills	Materials	Instrument	Pencil		
	Early Morning Attendance				

To take reporting of assessments one step further, a similar form (see figure 37) can be used to report to the district how your students performed on assessments. The difference between this form and the one in figure 36 is that the comment section is replaced by the four rubric levels. Insert the number of students at each level for each benchmark. Remember, most of your students will fall in level 3, some in levels 4 and 2, and a few in level 1.

Figure 37.
Critical Knowledge Portfolio/District Reporting

Grade 6 Orchestra Progress Report

Name _____

Grading period (circle one)   **1   2   3**

Rating Scale   4 = Exceeds expectations
3 = Expected at this grade level
2 = Working on this concept and progressing
1 = Beginning stages of development

Mark the number of
students at each level

Standard			Concept	Level 4	Level 3	Level 2	Level 1
1	Singing	1.8.1	Sings with accurate pitches and rhythms				
2	Performance	2.8.1	One octave scale				
		2.8.1	Correct posture and bow hold				
		2.8.1	Performs a variety of articulations				
		2.8.2	Performs expressively				
		2.8.3	Performs in an orchestra				
3	Improvisation	3.8.2	Improvises rhythmic variations				
		3.8.3	Improvises short melodies, given a set of notes and rhythms				
4	Composition	4.8.1	Composes simple ABA piece				
		4.8.2	Arranges accompaniment for melody with tonic and dominant chords				
5	Reading music	5.8.1	Labels rhythms				
		5.8.1	Labels notes				
		5.8.2	Sightreads simple melodies				
		5.8.3	Knows articulation notation				
		5.8.3	Knows dynamics notation				
6	Listening	6.8.1	Knows appropriate terminology to describe musical selections				
7	Evaluating music	7.8.1	Self-evaluation				
		7.8.2	Evaluates others positively				
8	Music and other subjects	8.8.1	Understands how emotions are portrayed in drama, visual art, and dance				
9	History and culture	9.8.1	Knows characteristics of a variety of music cultures				
		9.8.4	Proper audience behavior				
10	Care of instrument	10.8.1	Care of instrument and bow				
		10.8.2	Tunes with guidance				

REPORTING TO PARENTS: EMAIL, MIDTERMS, PROGRESS REPORTS, AND CONFERENCES

Email

Email is an excellent time-efficient way to communicate with parents. When you obtain student information at the beginning of the year, make sure to include a line for the parent's email address on the form.

Information to email:
1. Concert date reminders and changes
2. Student recordings such as SmartMusic® recordings, which are easily attached
3. Notification of tardiness or absence
4. Ideas for helping students with homework or practice
5. Community performances to attend
6. Great progress on learning targets
7. Extra help needed on learning targets

Midterm Progress Report

Grading software makes it very easy to send home progress reports. Some schools mail them, and other schools have students take them home for a parent signature. These can be mailed or emailed to parents. Some teachers require a parent signature. Be cautious of giving extra points for signatures returned. Grades should only include evidence of student learning.

Quarterly Progress Reports

Sharing progress with parents and students quarterly is important. No matter what device is used, feedback is valuable to your students and the music program. If a computerized version is not available, make sure you use a reporting system that makes recording information quick and easy.

Conference

Most districts have conferences once or twice a year. This is a great time to discuss student progress with parents. Using individual grading sheets labeled by standards shows parents specific progress toward each benchmark assessed. It also educates them about music standards and benchmarks.

PORTFOLIOS

Portfolios exhibit a student's expressive nature, performance, growth, evidence of achievement, and complex thinking over time. Putting together the housing for a portfolio takes time for the teacher who first instructs the student. The portfolio device is then passed on from teacher to teacher. Elementary teachers will pass general music portfolios to the teacher who has those students the next year. Instrumental and choral teachers will pass them from director to director.

File folders labeled with the student's name can be housed in a plastic crate or box for easy storage. Plastic stacking crates with wheels are very handy for transport to conference sites. Every teacher and school has different needs. Check out storage systems at local business supply dealers for easy storage and transport ideas. Electronic portfolios are ideal for recording and storing student work.

Included in the portfolio:
1. CD recordings of personal performances
2. Compositions (handwritten and/or electronic)
3. Theory worksheets
4. Word banks
5. Written assessments (pretests and post tests)
6. Personal essays on performances (self and others)
7. Personal evaluations of work ethic and attitude
8. Teacher evaluations
9. Peer evaluations
10. Record of activities in which the student is involved
11. Projects (pictures taken of projects or materials on a CD-ROM)
12. Programs of concerts in which the student had a special solo or recognition

When report cards are not electronically produced, make a copy of handwritten report cards for the portfolio for each quarter a student is in your class.

Audio software makes it easy to record personal performances which may be saved over a period of time and used to produce an audio CD. Be aware of copyright issues in recording group performances.

Examples of chunking standards-based activities and assessments for inclusion in a portfolio are:
1. Compositions (handwritten or produced with computer software)
2. A recording of the student performing it.
    a. If students produce a composition they cannot perform, another student or the teacher could record it.

What happens to the portfolios over time? They are used at conferences to show parents examples of student work, reviewed by teachers the students will have in the future, viewed by administrators and supervisors to see a snapshot of what is going on in the classroom and for students to keep at graduation. Examples of later high school work can be reviewed by college personnel for examples of the student's achievement in particular areas such as performance, composition, and theory.

Chapter 9

Student Involvement

NO CHILD LEFT BEHIND—LITERALLY

The No Child Left Behind bill requires that all students, regardless of race, intelligence, handicap, or socio-economic status strive for one-hundred-percent proficiency on state and national tests.

While we all know this is very difficult to accomplish, it does challenge educators and students to improve and continue to improve over time.

Instructors need to teach all of the children in the classroom, not the top ten percent that are responsive to the teacher. They need to respond to students who are not as talented as others and those that lack motivation. By writing a highly sequenced, standards-based curriculum, students begin to see music unfold. It begins to make sense to them and they become successful.

Another great way to give individual attention to all students is at the time of the assessment. Offer feedback and give students a chance to improve and offer their own feedback. At assessment time, teachers have an opportunity to make a connection with students and show that they care about them doing their best. When students know the teacher cares, they will care as well.

THE STUDENT'S OWNERSHIP IN EDUCATION

Offer opportunities for students to assess themselves. Whether educators like it or not, when there is a personality conflict, it is hard to assess without a biased opinion entering the mix. Students are often harder on themselves than teachers are when assessing.

After students have self-assessed, offer them an opportunity to create an improvement plan or another opportunity to try again to improve. Make sure students know it is okay to make a mistake in music class. That is everyone's goal—to practice and to improve. Mistakes are only opportunities for learning, and students need to feel comfortable in the classroom to experiment and improve. Wanting to improve is a skill that needs to be taught. When students want to do better, they begin to take ownership in their education.

SELF-ASSESSMENT

Make sure students have a copy of assessment forms prior to assessing so they know exactly what they are being graded on. While looking at the scoring rubric after the assessment, ask students to choose the rubric statements that apply to their assessment. Discuss with the student points on which you agree and disagree and why.

Offer students opportunities to reflect on their most recent performance (group or individual), making sure they have the tools (word bank) to be specific about what they did well, what needs improvement, and to create a plan to improve.

Students should have a continuous word bank that encourages them to spell and pronounce terms correctly. It is permissible to assess students on spelling and pronunciation so that they are able to speak and write intelligently about music.

Lastly, have students help you write a performance rubric to use during the school year. Students understand more than we give them credit for. When asked their opinion or assistance, they will take the job seriously and are usually very insightful of the goal.

Sometimes students are asked to participate in a cooperative work group. This a good time for students to evaluate how they work as a group. The following is a Likert scale which offers words to describe statements provided.

4. Always
3. Usually
2. Sometimes
1. Never

This also gives students an opportunity to explain why they did or did not work well as a group, what they like about their project and what they might change about it if given the opportunity. It may become evident that one student had an excellent idea that the rest of the students dismissed. Once students have determined what they may want to do over again, allow them the time to redo the project or presentation and use the grade from this second attempt. This process teaches students to think more in-depth and use these skills next time without the need to redo the activity.

Figure 38.
Elementary Cooperative Group Assessment

Elementary Cooperative Group Assessment

Name_____

Other Group Members

_____

_____

_____

_____

4 = Always   3 = Usually   2 = Sometimes   1 = Never

**Answer each statement with the appropriate number
that best describes how your group worked.**

_____ 1. Each person did their assigned job.

_____ 2. We shared equally in the work.

_____ 3. Our group followed the directions.

_____ 4. Our group completed the project on time.

_____ 5. Our group was cooperative.

If your group did not follow directions or complete the project, explain why.

What do you like best about your completed project?

What would you change about your completed project if you could?

STUDENTS ASSESSING OTHERS

When students assess each other, for example, on posture or performance, ask them to use comments with positive wording. "Here is what you did well..." or "Next time, try..."

When students have the words to specifically describe what they hear and see, they remember these points and begin to assess themselves in a similar fashion. Teach this skill to students by insisting they use correct spellings and know definitions of musical terms. Teach them what to look for in a performance. Never allow the statements such as "It was good," or "That was horrible." Teach students to be specific regarding feedback, just as teachers need to be specific.

STUDENT REPORTING

If your district has standards-based report cards, teach students how to interpret and explain these to their parents. Teach them what standards and benchmarks are and how to interpret rubrics and scores.. If every subject has a standards-based reporting system, parents can be overwhelmed with papers and scores. A simple education given to students will help narrow the gap of confusion with parents.

Have students attend their conferences. Both teacher and student can offer feedback on what has gone well for the quarter and what needs improvement. This also reinforces students' interpretation of their progress.

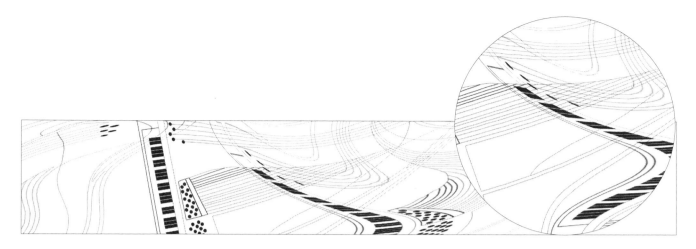

Chapter 10

Curriculum Sample

The following curriculum sample is for orchestra grades 5–12.

The benchmark numbers indicate:

1.8.1   a.   The first 1 indicates the first standard.

    b.   The 8 indicates alignment with the benchmarks for the national standards for grades 4–8.

    c.   The last 1 indicates the first benchmark.

For each benchmark learning targets or specific knowledge and performance tasks are listed by grade level.

  In a benchmark listing such as 1.E.1, E (for "exit") indicates alignment with the benchmarks for the national standards for grades 9–12.

  On the district level, the middle number can the grade level.

Figure 39.

Sample Orchestra Curriculum

1	SINGING
	Sing alone and with others, a varied repertoire of music

| **1.8.1 Sing accurately and with good breath control throughout the singing range, alone and in small and large groups** |

Grade	Learning Target (Specific Knowledge)	Performance Tasks
5	Demonstrate ability to sing in tune with good rhythm	1 Vocally echo a two-to-four-beat melody demonstrated by teacher 2 Sing question-and-answer statements 3 Sing phrases before playing

Grade	Learning Target (Specific Knowledge)	Performance Tasks
6	Demonstrate ability to sing in tune with good rhythm	1 Vocally echo a four-to-eight-beat melody demonstrated by teacher. 2 Sing question-and-answer statements 3 Sing phrases before playing

Grade	Learning Target (Specific Knowledge)	Performance Tasks
7	Demonstrate ability to sing in tune with good rhythm	1 Vocally echo a four-to-eight-beat melody demonstrated by teacher. 2 Sing question-and-answer statements 3 Sing phrases before playing

Grade	Learning Target (Specific Knowledge)	Performance Tasks
8	Demonstrate ability to sing in tune with good rhythm	1 Sing phrases before playing 2 Sing intervals a major and minor thirds b perfect fourths and fifths

| **1.E.1 Sing accurately and with good breath control throughout the singing range, alone and in small and large groups** |

Grade	Learning Target (Specific Knowledge)	Performance Tasks
9	Sing with pitch accuracy	1 Vocally match given tuning pitch or intervals

Grade	Learning Target (Specific Knowledge)	Performance Tasks
9	Vocally match: a legato e dynamics b staccato f style c accent g tempo variations d phrasing	1 Vocally match articulations and other musical concepts as demonstrated 2 Read and vocalize articulations and other musical concepts from an excerpt

Grade	Learning Target (Specific Knowledge)	Performance Tasks
9	Vocally match rhythms in unison	1 Vocally match rhythms as demonstrated by teacher

Grade	Learning Target (Specific Knowledge)	Performance Tasks
10	Vocally match: a specific pitches b intervals c tuning pitches	1 Listen to and sing selected instrumental excerpts and interval studies 2 Read and vocalize articulations and other musical concepts from an excerpt 3 Vocally match tuning notes
10	Vocally match: a legato e dynamics b staccato f style c accent g tempo variations d phrasing	1 Vocally match articulations and other musical concepts as demonstrated by teacher 2 Read and vocalize articulations and other musical concepts from an excerpt
10	Vocally match rhythms in unison and in parts	1 Vocally match rhythms as demonstrated by teacher 2 Read and vocalize rhythms from an excerpt
11	Vocally match: a specific pitches b intervals c tuning pitches	1 Listen to and sing selected instrumental excerpts and interval studies 2 Read and vocalize intervals 3 Vocally match tuning notes
11	Vocally match: a legato e dynamics b staccato f style c accent g tempo variations d phrasing	1 Vocally match articulations and other musical concepts as demonstrated by teacher 2 Read and vocalize articulations and other musical concepts from an excerpt
11	Vocally match rhythms in unison and parts	1 Vocally match rhythms as demonstrated 2 Read and vocalize rhythms from an excerpt
12	Vocally match: a specific pitches b intervals c tuning pitches	1 Listen to and sing selected instrumental excerpts and interval studies 2 Read and vocalize intervals 3 Vocally match tuning notes
12	Vocally match: a legato e dynamics b staccato f style c accent g tempo variations d phrasing	1 Vocally match articulations and other musical concepts as demonstrated 2 Read and vocalize articulations and other musical concepts from an excerpt

Grade	Learning Target (Specific Knowledge)	Performance Tasks
12	Vocally match rhythms in unison and parts	1 Vocally match rhythms as demonstrated
		2 Read and vocalize rhythms from an excerpt

2 INSTRUMENTAL PERFORMANCE
Perform on instruments, alone and with others, a varied repertoire of music

2.8.1   Perform on an instrument, alone and in small and large groups

Grade	Learning Target (Specific Knowledge)	Performance Tasks
5	Understand blend, tempo, and group dynamics of cooperation while playing within a group	1 Perform in a small or large ensemble with two to five independent parts
6	Understand blend, tempo, and group dynamics of cooperation while playing within a group	1 Perform in a small or large ensemble with two to five independent parts
7	Understand blend, tempo, and group dynamics of cooperation while playing within a group	1 Perform in a small or large ensemble with two to five independent parts
8	Understand blend, tempo, and group dynamics of cooperation while playing within a group	1 Perform in a small or large ensemble with two to five independent parts

2.8.2   Perform with expression and technical accuracy on a string, wind, percussion, or classroom instrument

Grade	Learning Target (Specific Knowledge)	Performance Tasks
5	Demonstrate dynamic and tempo changes along with proper bow usage	1 Perform Grade 1/2 to 1 literature or exercises which demonstrate dynamic and tempo changes along with proper bow usage

Grade	Learning Target (Specific Knowledge)	Performance Tasks

5	Perform with:
	
	a proper posture
	b position
	c tone
	d technique
	    1 bow directions 5 LH pizzicato
	       down bow 6 staccato
	       up bow 7 legato
	    2 two-to-three-
	       note slurs
	    3 arco
	    4 pizzicato
	
	bassists begin to shift
		1 Perform a Grade 1/2 to 1 piece or exercise in unison or individually
		
		2 Perform one-octave D, G, and C major scales in various styles, articulations, and tempos
		
		3 Bassists begin to shift to II–1/2 and III positions

6	Demonstrate dynamic and tempo changes along with phrasing	1 Perform Grade 1 to 1–1/2 literature or exercises which demonstrate dynamic and tempo changes along with phrasing and proper bow usage

6	Perform with:
	
	a proper posture
	b position
	c tone
	d technique
	e style
	    1 bow directions
	    2 technique
	       a détaché e double stops
	       b staccato f string
	       c two-to-four- crossings
	          note slurs g accents
	       d hooked
	          bowings
		1 Perform a Grade 1 to 1–1/2 piece or exercise in unison or individually
		
		2 Perform one-octave D, G, C, F, and B-flat major scales and related natural minor scales in various styles, articulations, and tempos
		
		3 Bassists begin to shift to 1/2 and II positions

7	Demonstrate dynamic and tempo changes along with phrasing and proper bow usage	1 Perform Grade 1–1/2 to 2–1/2 literature or exercises which demonstrate dynamic and tempo changes along with phrasing and proper bow usage

Grade	Learning Target (Specific Knowledge)	Performance Tasks
7	Perform with: a proper posture b position c tone d technique 　1 détaché　　　6 double stops 　2 marcato　　　7 string 　3 staccato　　　　 crossings 　4 four-to-eight-　8 accents 　　 note slurs　　9 spiccato 　5 hooked　　 10 tremolo 　　 bowings violinists, violists, and cellists begin to shift	1 Perform a Grade 1–1/2 to 2–1/2 piece or exercise in unison or alone 2 Perform one-octave D, G, C, F, B-flat, and A major scales and related natural minor scales in various styles, articulations, and tempos 3 Begin pre-vibrato string dusting 4 Begin pre-vibrato string dusting
8	Demonstrate dynamic and tempo changes along with proper phrasing, interpretation, and bow usage	1 Perform Grade 2 to 3 literature or exercises which demonstrate dynamic and tempo changes along with proper phrasing, interpretation, and bow usage
8	Perform with: a proper posture b position c tone d technique 　1 détaché　　　　8 accents 　2 marcato　　　　9 spiccato 　3 staccato　　 10 tremolo 　4 four-to-eight-　11 martele 　　 note slurs　　12 ponticello 　5 hooked　　 13 sul tasto 　　 bowings　　 14 loure 　6 double stops　15 shifting to 　7 string　　　　　 different 　　 crossings　　　　 positions	1 Perform a Grade 2 to 3 piece or exercise in unison or individually 2 Perform one-to-two octave D, G, C, F, B-flat, A, and E-flat major scale and related natural minor scales in various styles, articulations, and tempos 3 Perform octave harmonics 4 Demonstrate proper shifting techniques 5 Perform vibrato exercises with finger placed on the string using eighth, eighth-triplet, and sixteenth-note repetitions 6 Violinists and violists shift up to III position; cellists begin to shift to IV positions; bassists begin to shift to V position

2.8.3 Perform music representing diverse genres and cultures

Grade	Learning Target (Specific Knowledge)	Performance Tasks

5	Perform a variety of music:
	
	a folk music from a variety of cultures
	b music of great composers from all eras
	c introduction to contemporary music, including elements of:
	  1 blues 3 country
	  2 jazz 4 pieces involving improvisation
		1 Perform Grade 1/2 to 1 literature or excerpts of literature from various cultures, eras, and musical styles

6	Perform a variety of music:
	
	a folk music from a variety of cultures
	b music of great composers from all eras
	c introduction to contemporary music, including elements of:
	  1 blues 3 country
	  2 jazz 4 pieces involving improvisation
		1 Perform Grade 1 to 1–1/2 literature or excerpts of literature from various cultures, eras, and musical styles

7	Perform a variety of music:
	a folk music from a variety of cultures
	b music of great composers from all eras
	c introduction to contemporary music, including elements of:
	  1 blues 3 country
	  2 jazz 4 pieces involving improvisation
		1 Perform Grade 1–1/2 to 2–1/2 literature or excerpts of literature from various cultures, eras, and musical styles

8	Perform a variety of music:
	
	a folk music from a variety of cultures
	b music of great composers from all eras
	c introduction to contemporary music, including elements of:
	  1 blues 3 country
	  2 jazz 4 pieces involving improvisation
		1 Perform Grade 2 to 3 literature or excerpts of literature from various cultures, eras, and musical styles

2.E.1 Perform with expression and technical accuracy

Grade	Learning Target (Specific Knowledge)	Performance Tasks
9	Demonstrate: a listening e interpretation b rubato f various meters c dynamics g rhythms in a d phrasing variety of keys	1 Apply knowledge of expression, tone quality, and technical accuracy through performance of literature alone or in groups; describe and support interpretations of this literature 2 Perform one-to-two octave scales and literature in major and minor keys of up to three flats or sharps

9	Understand and demonstrate:
	
	a vibrato e tone
	b articulation f style
	c proper g intonation
	   posture
	d playing in
	   positions
		1 Demonstrate proper position, posture, and playing technique using current repertoire
		
		2 Violinists play up to V positions
		
		3 Violists play up to V positions
		
		4 Cellists play up to IV position
		
		5 Bassists play up to V position

10	Demonstrate:
	
	a rubato d interpretation
	b dynamics e various meters
	c phrasing f rhythms in a
	              variety of keys
	              and styles
		1 Perform an assigned piece, alone or with others, to develop concepts and skills of expression, tone quality, and technical accuracy in major and minor keys of up to three sharps and three flats
		
		2 Perform two-to-three-octave scales representative of performance literature
		
		3 Respond to musical markings with adequate flexibility to conductor or performing group

10	Understand and demonstrate:
	
	a vibrato e tone
	b articulation f style
	c proper g intonation
	   posture
	d playing in
	   positions
		1 Demonstrate proper position, posture, and playing techniques using current repertoire

11	Demonstrate:
	
	a rubato d interpretation
	b dynamics e various meters
	c phrasing f rhythms in a
	              variety of keys
	              and styles
		1 Perform an assigned piece, alone or with others, to develop concepts and skills of expression, tone quality, and technical accuracy in major and minor keys of up to four sharps or flats
		
		2 Perform two-to-three-octave scales representative of performance literature
		
		3 Respond to musical markings with adequate flexibility to conductor or performing group

Grade	Learning Target (Specific Knowledge)	Performance Tasks

11	Understand and demonstrate:
	
	a vibrato e tone
	b articulation f style
	c proper g intonation
	   posture
	d playing in
	   positions
		1 Demonstrate proper position, posture, and playing techniques using current repertoire

11	Demonstrate:
	
	a rubato d interpretation
	b dynamics e various meters
	c phrasing f rhythms in a
	              variety of keys
	              and styles
		1 Perform an assigned piece, alone or with others, to develop concepts and skills of expression, tone quality, and technical accuracy in major and minor keys of up to four sharps or flats
		
		2 Perform two-to-three-octave scales representative of performance literature
		
		3 Respond to musical markings with adequate flexibility to conductor or performing group

12	Understand and demonstrate:
	
	a vibrato e tone
	b articulation f style
	c proper g intonation
	   posture
	d playing in
	   positions
		1 Demonstrate proper position, posture, and playing techniques using current repertoire

2.E.2 Perform in an ensemble

Grade	Learning Target (Specific Knowledge)	Performance Tasks
9	Practice ensemble skills: a balance c rhythmic unity b intonation d tone	1 Learn and practice the elements of music and independence of line to perform their parts in an ensemble experience
10	Demonstrate ensemble skills: a balance d tone b intonation e interpretations c rhythmic unity f score reading	1 Use knowledge of the elements of music and independence of line to perform their parts in an ensemble experience
11	Demonstrate ensemble skills: a balance d tone b intonation e interpretation c rhythmic unity f score reading	1 Use knowledge of the elements of music and independence of line to perform their parts in an ensemble experience

Grade	Learning Target (Specific Knowledge)		Performance Tasks
12	Demonstrate ensemble skills: a balance d tone b intonation e interpretation c rhythmic unity f score reading	1	Use knowledge of the elements of music and independence of line to perform their parts in an ensemble experience

2.E.3 Perform in small ensembles with one on a part

Grade	Learning Target (Specific Knowledge)		Performance Tasks
9	Demonstrate musical independence, listening skills, blending, and cooperation	1	Perform in a small ensemble of two to twelve people with one person per part a the ensemble plays without a conductor and unaccompanied b the literature is comparable to Grade 3 literature
10	Demonstrate: a musical c blending independence d cooperation b listening skills	1	Perform in a small ensemble of two to twelve people with one person per part a the ensemble plays without a conductor and unaccompanied b the literature is comparable to Grade 3 to 3–1/2 literature
11	Demonstrate: a musical c blending independence d cooperation b listening skills	1	Perform in a small ensemble of two to twelve people with one person per part a the ensemble plays without a conductor and unaccompanied b the literature is comparable to Grade 3–1/2 to 4 literature
12	Demonstrate: a musical c blending independence d cooperation b listening skills	1	Perform in a small ensemble of 2 to 12 people with one person per part a the ensemble plays without a conductor and unaccompanied b the literature is comparable to Grade 4 to 5 literature

3 IMPROVISATION
Improvise melodies, variations, and accompaniments

3.8.1 Improvise simple harmonic accompaniments

Grade	Learning Target (Specific Knowledge)		Performance Tasks
5	Improvise an accompaniment based on tonic and dominant tones given while another student, group, or teacher plays a melody	1	Listen and determine when chords change in a basic accompaniment
		2	Determine the tonic and dominant tones for an accompaniment to a simple melody and make proper changes using a rhythm pattern used in the accompanied melody

Grade	Learning Target (Specific Knowledge)		Performance Tasks
6	Improvise an accompaniment based on root of the tonic and dominant chord given while another student, group, or teacher plays a melody	1	Determine the root tone of the tonic and dominant chords for an accompaniment to a simple melody and make proper chord changes using a rhythm pattern of choice
7	Improvise an accompaniment based on root of the tonic, subdominant, and dominant chords given while another student, group, or teacher plays a melody	1	Determine where chord changes occur while improvising an accompaniment to a simple melody and make proper chord changes using a rhythmic pattern of choice
8	Improvise an accompaniment based on the tonic, subdominant, and dominant triads while another student, group, or teacher plays a melody	1	Determine where chord changes occur while improvising an accompaniment to a simple melody and make proper chord changes using a rhythmic pattern of choice

3.8.2 Improvise melodic embellishments and simple rhythmic and melodic variations

Grade	Learning Target (Specific Knowledge)		Performance Tasks
5	Understand the techniques of changing the rhythmic structure of a simple given melody	1	Improvise rhythmic variations on a previously learned exercise in the method book
6	Understand the techniques of changing the rhythmic structure of a simple given melody	1	Improvise rhythmic variations on a previously learned exercise in the method book
7	Improvise melodic embellishments and simple rhythmic and melodic variations on given pentatonic melodies and melodies in major keys	1	Improvise a melodic variation using neighboring or chordal tones on a given or original melody
8	Improvise melodic embellishments and simple rhythmic and melodic variations on given pentatonic melodies and melodies in major keys	1	Improvise simple rhythmic or melodic variations with specific directions on a given or original melody

3.8.3 Improvise short melodies, unaccompanied and over given rhythmic accompaniments

Grade	Learning Target (Specific Knowledge)	Performance Tasks
5	Understand how to mix and improvise given notes and rhythms in a steady tempo with or without accompaniment a quarter note and rest b eighth note and rest c half note and rest d whole note and rest e dotted half note f tied notes in 2/4, 3/4, and 4/4 meters	1 Improvise a melody using a given set of notes and rhythms
6	Understand how to mix and improvise given notes and rhythms in a steady tempo with or without accompaniment a quarter note and rest b eighth note and rest c sixteenth note d dotted eighth note e eighth note triplet f dotted quarter note g half note and rest h whole note and rest i dotted half note j syncopated rhythms using eighth-quarter-eighth k tied notes l combinations of these note values in 2/4, 3/4, 4/4, and 6/8 meters	1 Improvise a melody using a given set of notes and rhythms
7	Understand how to mix and improvise given notes and rhythms in a steady tempo with or without accompaniment (e.g., quarter note and quarter rest; eighth note and eighth rest; sixteenth note; dotted eighth note; eighth note triplet; dotted quarter note and dotted quarter rest; half note and half rest; whole note and whole rest; dotted half note; syncopated rhythms using eighth-quarter-eighth or sixteenth-eighth-sixteenth; tied notes; and combinations of the above mentioned note values in in 2/4, 3/4, 4/4, 2/2, 3/8, and 6/8 meters	1 Understand how to mix known notes and rhythms in a steady tempo with or without accompaniment

Grade	Learning Target (Specific Knowledge)		Performance Tasks
8	Understand how to mix and improvise given notes and rhythms in a steady tempo with or without accompaniment (e.g., quarter note and quarter rest; eighth note and eighth rest; sixteenth note; dotted eighth note; eighth note triplet; dotted quarter note and dotted quarter rest; half note and half rest; whole note and whole rest; dotted half note; syncopated rhythms using eighth-quarter-eighth or sixteenth-eighth-sixteenth; tied notes; and combinations of the above mentioned note values in in 2/4, 3/4, 4/4, 2/2, 3/8, 6/8 and 5/8 meters	1	Understand how to mix known notes and rhythms in a steady tempo with or without accompaniment

3.E.1 Improvise stylistically appropriate harmonizing parts

Grade	Learning Target (Specific Knowledge)		Performance Tasks
9	Understand and demonstrate harmonic progression (e.g., I, IV, and V chords and inversions) and stylistically appropriate to the melody supporting the melody, not excessively busy, reflecting the form of the melody and the text if possible	1	Given a familiar melody that uses at least three different chords,improvise an accompaniment on a suitable instrument There should be a chord on every strong beat The accompaniment should be stylistically appropriate to the melodyplay the accompaniment while the melody is provided by teacher, otheror a recording
10	Understand and demonstrate harmonic progression (e.g., I, IV, and V chords and inversions) and stylistically appropriate to the melody supporting the melody, not excessively busy, reflecting the form of the melody and the text if possible	1	Given a familiar melody that uses at least three different chords,improvise an accompaniment on a suitable instrument There should be a chord on every strong beat The accompaniment should be stylistically appropriate to the melodyplay the accompaniment while the melody is provided by teacher, otheror a recording
11	Understand and demonstrate harmonic progression (e.g., I, IV, and V chords and inversions) and stylistically appropriate to the melody supporting the melody, not excessively busy, reflecting the form of the melody and the text if possible	1	Given a familiar melody that uses at least three different chords,improvise an accompaniment on a suitable instrument There should be a chord on every strong beat The accompaniment should be stylistically appropriate to the melodyplay the accompaniment while the melody is provided by teacher, otheror a recording

Grade	Learning Target (Specific Knowledge)		Performance Tasks
12	Understand and demonstrate harmonic progression (e.g., I, IV, and V chords and inversions) and stylistically appropriate to the melody supporting the melody, not excessively busy, reflecting the form of the melody and the text if possible	1	Given a familiar melody that uses at least three different chords,improvise an accompaniment on a suitable instrument There should be a chord on every strong beat The accompaniment should be stylistically appropriate to the melodyplay the accompaniment while the melody is provided by teacher, otheror a recording

3.E.2 Improvise rhythmic and melodic variations

Grade	Learning Target (Specific Knowledge)		Performance Tasks
9	Improvise melodies in major and/or minor keys as well as rhythmic patterns	1	Improvise melodic variations on a short, familiar melody or melodic excerpt, with clearly implied chords The strategy should be repeated, withimprovising rhythmic variations An accompaniment may be providedmay use an instrument, object, body rhythm, or voice
10	Improvise melodies in major and/or minor keys and pentatonic melodies as well as rhythmic patterns	1	Improvise melodic variations on a short, familiar melody or melodic excerpt, with clearly implied chords The strategy should be repeated, withimprovising rhythmic variations An accompaniment may be providedmay use an instrument, object, body rhythm, or voice
11	Improvise melodies in major and/or minor keys, modal scales, and pentatonic melodies as well as rhythm patterns	1	Improvise melodic variations on a short, familiar melody or melodic excerpt, with clearly implied chords The strategy should be repeated, withimprovising rhythmic variations An accompaniment may be providedmay use an instrument, object, body rhythm, or voice
12	Improvise melodies in major and/or minor keys, modal scales, and pentatonic melodies as well as rhythm patterns	1	Improvise melodic variations on a short, familiar melody or melodic excerpt, with clearly implied chords The strategy should be repeated, withimprovising rhythmic variations An accompaniment may be providedmay use an instrument, object, body rhythm, or voice

3.E.3 Improvise original melodies over given chord progressions

Grade	Learning Target (Specific Knowledge)		Performance Tasks
9	Improvise using consistent style, meter, and tonality (e.g., a 12-bar blues progression	1	Improvise a 4 to 12 measure melody using given or chosen tones and rhythms over a set chord progression
10	Improvise using consistent style, meter, and tonality (e.g., a 12-bar blues progression	1	Improvise a 4 to 12 measure melody using given or chosen tones and rhythms over a set chord progression
11	Improvise using consistent style, meter, and tonality (e.g., a 12-bar blues progression	1	Improvise a 4 to 12 measure melody using given or chosen tones and rhythms over a set chord progression
12	Improvise using consistent style, meter, and tonality (e.g., a 12-bar blues progression	1	Improvise a 4 to 12 measure melody using given or chosen tones and rhythms over a set chord progression

4 COMPOSITION
Students compose and arrange music with specified guidelines

4.8.1 Compose short pieces containing the appropriate elements of music

Grade	Learning Target (Specific Knowledge)		Performance Tasks
5	Understand basic rules of notation	1	Compose or complete a simple melody using given tones and rhythms paying close attention to note placement and stem direction
6	Understand basic rules of notation, dynamics, phrasing, and form	1	Compose or complete a simple melody using given tones and rhythms in a simple ABA form
7	Understand basic rules of notation, dynamics, phrasing, and form	1	Compose or complete a simple melody using given tones and rhythms in a simple ABA form with the addition of A1 or B1 sections
8	Understand basic rules of notation, dynamics, phrasing, form, and instrumentation	1	Compose or complete a simple melody with a one line accompaniment by another orchestral instrument

4.8.2 Arrange simple pieces for voices or instruments other than those for which the pieces were written

Grade	Learning Target (Specific Knowledge)		Performance Tasks
5	Understand basic tonic and dominant chord changes	1	Arrange a simple one note accompaniment to a given or original melody using the tonic and dominant tones of the chord
6	Understand instrument voicing for their own and other instruments within large and small ensemble pieces	1	Arrange an eight measure duet using the instrument they play and a different instrument than the one they play
7	Understand the range of their instrument and how to make a pre-existing melody fit in that range	1	Arrange a melodic fragment from another instrument in the orchestra to fit their instrument (choose from a piece being studied in large group orchestra)
8	Understand tonic, subdominant, and dominant chord changes and inversions	1	Arrange an accompaniment to a given melody for two-four orchestral instruments using tonic, subdominant, and dominant chords and their inversions

4.E.1 Compose music in several distinct styles

Grade	Learning Target (Specific Knowledge)		Performance Tasks
9	Notate music with proper range, harmony, creativity, and instrumentation in styles (e.g., classical, jazz, fiddling, or folk	1	Compose a short work for an ensemble and then write two contrasting styles of the same workexchange compositions and perform them
10	Notate music with proper range, harmony, timbre, creativity, and instrumentation in styles (e.g., classical, jazz, fiddling, or folk	1	Compose a short work for an ensemble and then write two contrasting styles of the same workexchange compositions and perform them
11	Notate music with expressive effects, proper range, harmony, timbre, creativity, and instrumentation in styles (e.g., classical, jazz, fiddling, or folk	1	Compose a short work for an ensemble and then write two contrasting styles of the same workexchange compositions and perform them
12	Notate music with expressive effects, proper range, harmony, timbre, creativity, and instrumentation in styles (e.g., classical, jazz, fiddling, or folk	1	Compose a short work for an ensemble and then write two contrasting styles of the same workexchange compositions and perform them

4.E.2 Arrange pieces for voices or instruments other than those for which the pieces were written in ways that preserve or enhance the expressive effect of the music

Grade	Learning Target (Specific Knowledge)		Performance Tasks
9	Notate music with proper range, harmony, and instrumentation	1	Arrange an existing work which is to be notated and performed An example would be a rock song arranged for string quartet or vocal solo arranged as a string duet
10	Notate music with proper range, harmony, timbre, creativity, and instrumentation	1	Arrange an existing work which is to be notated and performed An example would be a rock song arranged for string quartet or vocal solo arranged as a string duet
11	Notate music with expressive effects, proper range, harmony, timbre, creativity, and instrumentation	1	Arrange an existing work which is to be notated and performed An example would be a rock song arranged for string quartet or vocal solo arranged as a string duet
12	Notate music with expressive effects, proper range, harmony, timbre, creativity, and instrumentation	1	Arrange an existing work which is to be notated and performed An example would be a rock song arranged for string quartet or vocal solo arranged as a string duet

5 READING MUSIC
Students read and notate music

5.8.1 Read complex rhythms in simple and compound meters

Grade	Learning Target (Specific Knowledge)		Performance Tasks
5	Demonstrate an understanding of the following rhythmic durations and related rests in 2/4, 3/4, and 4/4 meter - quarter note and quarter rest: eighth note and eighth rest; half note and half rest; whole note and whole rest; dotted half note and tied notes	1	Clap and count, label or play rhythms accurately using familiar or unfamiliar flash cards, exercises, or excerpts in current literature
6	Demonstrate an understanding of the following rhythmic durations and related rests in 2/4, 3/4, 4/4, 2/2, 3/8, and 6/8 meters - quarter note and quarter rest; eighth note and eighth rest; sixteenth note; dotted eighth note; eighth note triplet; dotted quarter note; half note and half rest; whole note and whole rest; dotted half note; syncopated rhythms using eighth-quarter-eighth, tied notes, and combinations of the above mentioned note values	1	Clap and count, label or play rhythms accurately using familiar or unfamiliar flash cards, exercises, or excerpts in current literature

Grade	Learning Target (Specific Knowledge)		Performance Tasks
7	Demonstrate an understanding of the following rhythmic durations and related rests in 2/4, 3/4, 4/4, 2/2, 3/8, and 6/8 meters - quarter note and quarter rest; eighth note and eighth rest; sixteenth note; dotted eighth note; eighth note triplet; dotted quarter note; half note and half rest; whole note and whole rest; dotted half note; syncopated rhythms using eighth-quarter-eighth or sixteenth-eighth-sixteenth; tied notes, and combinations of the above mentioned note values	1	Clap and count, label or play rhythms accurately using familiar or unfamiliar flash cards, exercises, or excerpts in current literature

Grade	Learning Target (Specific Knowledge)		Performance Tasks
8	Demonstrate an understanding of the following rhythmic durations and related rests in 2/4, 3/4, 4/4, 2/2, 3/8, 6/8, and 5/8 meters - quarter note and quarter rest; eighth note and eighth rest; sixteenth note; dotted eighth note; eighth note triplet; dotted quarter note and dotted quarter rest; half note and half rest; whole note and whole rest; dotted half note; syncopated rhythms using eighth-quarter-eighth or sixteenth-eighth-sixteenth; tied notes, and combinations of the above mentioned note values	1	Clap and count, label or play rhythms accurately using familiar or unfamiliar flash cards, exercises, or excerpts in current literature

5.8.2 Sight-read simple melodies in both the treble and bass clefs

Grade	Learning Target (Specific Knowledge)		Performance Tasks
5	Identify notes by letter names and fingerings in 1st position in the keys (e.g., D, G, or C major	1	Name or play accurate pitches in familiar or unfamiliar flash cards, exercises, or excerpts in current literature

Grade	Learning Target (Specific Knowledge)		Performance Tasks
6	Identifies notes by letter names in keys (e.g., D, G, C, and F and related minors	1	Name or play accurate pitches in familiar or unfamiliar flash cards, exercises, or excerpts in current literature

Grade	Learning Target (Specific Knowledge)		Performance Tasks
7	Name transfer notes from their clef to another clef (treble, alto and bass)	1	Name or play accurate pitches in familiar or unfamiliar flash cards, exercises, or excerpts in current literature

Grade	Learning Target (Specific Knowledge)		Performance Tasks
7	Identify half and whole steps in relation to finger charts or finger patterns	1	Label and play intervals of half or whole step in a scale or musical excerpt

Grade	Learning Target (Specific Knowledge)		Performance Tasks
8	Identify notes by letter names and fingerings in I and III position for violin and viola and I through IV positions for cello and bass	1	Name and play accurate pitches shifting from I to III position for violin and viola and I to IV positions for cello and bass, with a smooth, relaxed transition from position to position

Grade	Learning Target (Specific Knowledge)		Performance Tasks
8	Identify half and whole steps in relation to finger charts or finger patterns in more than one position	1	Label and play intervals of half or whole step in more than one position in a scale or musical excerpt

5.8.3 Know standard notation symbols

Grade	Learning Target (Specific Knowledge)		Performance Tasks
5	Identify standard symbols used to notate meter, rhythm, pitch, bowings, dynamics, and style	1	Demonstrate how to notate symbols and note placement through their own composition and/or worksheets
	a 2/4, 3/4, and 4/4 meters	2	Students compose a warm-up exercise addressing a rhythm, articulation, key signature or dynamics learned
	b quarter note and rest; eighth note and rest; half note and rest; whole note and whole rest; dotted half note and tied notes	3	Write major scales on the staff
	c notes in the keys of D, G, and C major		
	d symbols for down bow, up bow, slurs, arco, pizzicato, and LH pizzicato		
	e piano and forte, crescendo and decrescendo		
	f legato and staccato		

Grade	Learning Target (Specific Knowledge)	Performance Tasks
6	Identify standard symbols used to notate meter, rhythm, pitch, bowings, dynamics, and style	1 Demonstrate how to notate symbols and note placement through their own composition and/or worksheets
	a 2/4, 3/4, 4/4, and 6/8 meters	2 Compose a warm-up exercise addressing a rhythm, articulation, key signature or dynamics learned
	b quarter note and rest; eighth note and rest; sixteenth note; dotted eighth note; eighth note triplet; dotted quarter note; half note and rest; whole note and rest; dotted half note; syncopated rhythms using eighth-quarter-eighth; tied notes; and combinations of the above mentioned note values	3 Write major and minor scales on the staff
	c notes in D, G, C, F, and B-flat major and related minor keys	
	d symbols for down bow, up bow, slurs, arco, pizzicato, and LH pizzicato	
	e piano, mezzo piano, forte, mezzo forte, crescendo, and decrescendo	
	f legato, staccato, détaché, hooked bowings, double stops, and accents	

7	Identify standard symbols used to notate meter, rhythm, pitch, bowings, dynamics and style:	1 Demonstrate how to notate symbols and note placement through their own composition and/or worksheets
	a 2/4, 3/4, 4/4, 2/2, 3/8, and 6/8 meters	2 Compose a warm-up exercise addressing a rhythm, articulation, key signature or dynamics learned
	b quarter note and rest; eighth note and rest; sixteenth note: dotted eighth note; eighth note triplet; dotted quarter note and rest; half note and rest; whole note and rest; dotted half note; syncopated rhythms using eighth-quarter-eighth or sixteenth-eighth-sixteenth; tied notes; and combinations of the above mentioned note values	3 Write major and minor scales on the staff
	c notes in D, G, C, F, B-flat, and A major and related minor keys	
	d symbols for down bow, up bow, slurs, arco, pizzicato, and LH pizzicato	
	e mezzo forte, forte, mezzo piano, piano, crescendo and decrescendo	
	f staccato, legato, détaché, hooked bowings, double stops, and accents	

Grade	Learning Target (Specific Knowledge)	Performance Tasks
8	Identify standard symbols used to notate meter, rhythm, pitch, bowings, dynamics and style:	1 Demonstrate how to notate symbols and note placement through their own composition and/or worksheets
	a 2/4, 3/4, 4/4, 2/2, 3/8, 6/8, and 5/8 meters	2 Compose a warm-up exercise addressing a rhythm, articulation, key signature or dynamics learned
	b quarter note and rest; eighth note and rest; sixteenth note; dotted eighth note; eighth note triplet; dotted quarter note and rest; half note and rest; whole note and rest; dotted half note; syncopated rhythms using eighth-quarter-eighth or sixteenth-eighth-sixteenth; tied notes; and combinations of the above mentioned note values	3 Write major and minor (natural, harmonic and melodic) scales on the staff
	c notes in D, G, C, F, B-flat, A, and E-flat major and related minor keys	
	d symbols for down bow, up bow, slurs, arco, pizzicato, and LH pizzicato	
	e crescendo, decrescendo, mezzo forte, forte, fortissimo, fortississimo, mezzo piano, piano, pianissimo and pianississimo	
	f staccato, legato, détaché, hooked bowings, double stops, accents, marcato, spiccato, and tremolo	

5.E.1 Know how to read a score of up to four staves

Grade	Learning Target (Specific Knowledge)	Performance Tasks
9	Label clefs, all musical terms and symbols, key signatures, time signatures, tempo markings, style markings, and articulations	1 Read and interpret a familiar or unfamiliar score of music

Grade	Learning Target (Specific Knowledge)	Performance Tasks
9	Use the score to identify entrances, or similar rhythms and melodies to problem solve in a small ensemble rehearsal	1 Read a score when rehearsing a small ensemble

Grade	Learning Target (Specific Knowledge)	Performance Tasks
10	Label clefs, all musical terms and symbols, key signatures, time signatures, tempo markings, style markings, and articulations	1 Read and interpret a familiar or unfamiliar score of music

Grade	Learning Target (Specific Knowledge)		Performance Tasks
10	Use the score to identify entrances, or similar rhythms and melodies to problem solve in a small ensemble rehearsal	1	Read a score when rehearsing a small ensemble
11	Label clefs, all musical terms and symbols, key signatures, time signatures, tempo markings, style markings, and articulations	1	Read and interpret a familiar or unfamiliar score of music
11	Use the score to identify entrances, or similar rhythms and melodies to problem solve in a small ensemble rehearsal	1	Read a score when rehearsing a small ensemble
12	Label clefs, all musical terms and symbols, key signatures, time signatures, tempo markings, style markings, and articulations	1	Read and interpret a familiar or unfamiliar score of music
12	Use the score to identify entrances, or similar rhythms and melodies to problem solve in a small ensemble rehearsal	1	Read a score when rehearsing a small ensemble
12	Understand transposition, instrumentation, clefs, all musical terms and symbols, and non-standard notation symbols	1	Identify and describe, using a score of current repertoire, form, relative importance of various lines, and identify transpositions and clefs

6   LISTENING
Students listen to, analyze, and describe music

6.8.1   Understand appropriate terminology to describe specific music events

Grade	Learning Target (Specific Knowledge)		Performance Tasks
5	Describe basic differences and similarities within a musical selection or between musical selections (e.g., fast/slow, loud/soft, high/low and repetition); identify forms of AB, ABA, and round	1	Compare and contrast sections within current repertoire or listening examples or between two musical selections
		2	Identify form through viewing, listening or playing a piece of music

Grade	Learning Target (Specific Knowledge)	Performance Tasks
6	Describe basic differences and similarities within a music selection or between musical selections (e.g., fast/slow, loud/soft, legato/staccato, repetition, and major/minor); identify AB, ABA, round, or canon form; aurally identify changes in tonality from major to minor	1 Compare and contrast sections within current repertoire or listening examples or between two musical selections 2 Identify form through viewing, listening, or playing a piece of music
7	Describe basic differences and similarities within a music selection or between musical selections (fast/slow, loud/soft, legato/staccato, repetition, major/minor, bowing styles, and instrumentation); identify AB, ABA, round, canon, and theme and variations forms); aurally identify changes in tonality from major to minor; identify the intervals perfect fourth, perfect fifth, and octave	1 Compare and contrast sections within current repertoire or listening examples or between two musical selections 2 Identify form through viewing, listening, or playing a piece of music
8	Describe basic differences and similarities within a music selection or between musical selections (fast/slow, loud/soft, legato/staccato, repetition, major/minor, bowing styles, instrumentation, and type of composition) identify AB, ABA, round, canon, and theme and variations forms; aurally identify changes in tonality from major to minor; identify the intervals perfect fourth, perfect fifth, and octave	1 Compare and contrast sections within current repertoire or listening examples or between two musical selections 2 Identify form through viewing, listening or playing a piece of music

6.8.2 Know the uses of the elements of music in the analysis of compositions representing diverse genres and cultures

Grade	Learning Target (Specific Knowledge)	Performance Tasks
5	Understand and identify the elements of music from various genres and cultures that are readily discernible (genres could include folk song, fiddle tune, jazz, rock, and classical music)	1 Play or listen to examples of music from diverse genres and cultures and identify elements that distinguish one from another
6	Understand and identify the elements of music from various genres and cultures that are readily discernible (genres could include folk song, fiddle tune, jazz, rock, and classical music)	1 Play or listen to examples of music from diverse genres and cultures and identify elements that distinguish one from another

Grade	Learning Target (Specific Knowledge)		Performance Tasks
7	Understand and identify the elements of music from various genres and cultures that are readily discernible (genres could include folk song, fiddle tune, jazz, rock, and classical music)	1	Play or listen to examples of music from diverse genres and cultures and identify elements that distinguish one from another

Grade	Learning Target (Specific Knowledge)		Performance Tasks
8	Understand and identify the elements of music from various genres and cultures that are readily discernible (genres could include folk song, fiddle tune, jazz, rock, and classical music)	1	Play or listen to examples of music from diverse genres and cultures and identify elements that distinguish one from another

6.E.1 Know the uses of the elements of music in the analysis of compositions representing diverse genres and cultures

Grade	Learning Target (Specific Knowledge)		Performance Tasks
9	Identify musical elements, compositional devices, and techniques (e.g., motives, imitation, retrograde, inversion, or chromaticism)	1	Analyze or describe current repertoire or a written or recorded example
10	Identify and understand the elements of twelve-tone and polyphonic music	1	Analyze or describe current repertoire or a written or recorded example
11	Identify musical elements of bitonality	1	Analyze or describe current repertoire or a written or recorded example
12	Identify musical elements, Western and Non-Western tonality, and form (e.g., fugue, sonata, theme and variations, and rondo compared to Japanese, African, or other Asian music)	1	Analyze or describe current repertoire; listen to, compare, and contrast similar or contrasting styles of repertoire

6.E.2 Understand technical vocabulary of music

Grade	Learning Target (Specific Knowledge)		Performance Tasks
9	Identify and understand elements of music, tempo markings, English and non-English terms, harmony, form, and articulations	1	Construct an ongoing word bank to identify, discuss, or write elements of music using proper terminology

Grade	Learning Target (Specific Knowledge)		Performance Tasks
10	Identify and understand elements of music, tempo markings, English and non-English terms, harmony, form, and articulations	1	Construct an ongoing word bank to identify, discuss, or write elements of music using proper terminology

Grade	Learning Target (Specific Knowledge)		Performance Tasks
11	Identify and understand elements of music, tempo markings, English and non-English terms, harmony, form, and articulations	1	Construct an ongoing word bank to identify, discuss, or write elements of music using proper terminology

Grade	Learning Target (Specific Knowledge)		Performance Tasks
12	Identify and understand elements of music, tempo markings, English and non-English terms, harmony, form, and articulations	1	Construct an ongoing word bank to identify, discuss, or write elements of music using proper terminology

7 EVALUATING MUSIC
Students evaluate music and music performances

7.8.1 Know how to evaluate the quality and effectiveness of music and music performances

Grade	Learning Target (Specific Knowledge)		Performance Tasks
5	Understand basic elements of a successful performance by self or others (e.g., posture/position, tone quality, note and rhythm reading accuracy, intonation, and dynamics)	1	Evaluate a performance by self or others aurally or in written form

Grade	Learning Target (Specific Knowledge)		Performance Tasks
6	Understand basic elements of a successful performance by self or others (e.g., posture/position, tone quality, note and rhythm reading accuracy, intonation, dynamics, and articulation)	1	Evaluate a performance by self or others aurally or in written form

Grade	Learning Target (Specific Knowledge)		Performance Tasks
7	Understand basic elements of a successful performance by self or others (e.g., posture/position, tone quality, note and rhythm reading accuracy, intonation, dynamics, articulation, style, and precision of performance)	1	Evaluate a performance by self or others aurally or in written form

Grade	Learning Target (Specific Knowledge)	Performance Tasks
8	Understand basic elements of a successful performance by self or others (e.g., posture/position, tone quality, note and rhythm reading accuracy, intonation, dynamics, articulation, style, and precision of performance)	1 Evaluate a performance by self or others aurally or in written form
	Using appropriate terminology, explain personal preference for specific musical works and styles	2 Discuss personal preferences from a performance by self or others aurally or in written form

7.8.2 Know how to apply specific criteria when offering constructive suggestions for improving performance of self and others

Grade	Learning Target (Specific Knowledge)	Performance Tasks
5	Know vocabulary for giving and receiving feedback for improving performance of self and others	1 Offer both positive comments and constructive suggestions for improvement of a personal or group performance

Grade	Learning Target (Specific Knowledge)	Performance Tasks
6	Know vocabulary for giving and receiving feedback for improving performance of self and others	1 Offer both positive comments and constructive suggestions for improvement of a personal or group performance

Grade	Learning Target (Specific Knowledge)	Performance Tasks
7	Know vocabulary for giving and receiving feedback for improving performance of self and others	1 Offer both positive comments and constructive suggestions for improvement of a personal or group performance

Grade	Learning Target (Specific Knowledge)	Performance Tasks
8	Know vocabulary for giving and receiving feedback for improving performance of self and others	1 Offer both positive comments and constructive suggestions for improvement of a personal or group performance

7.E.1 Develop or apply specific criteria for making informed, critical evaluations of quality and effectiveness of performances, compositions, arrangements, and improvisations

Grade	Learning Target (Specific Knowledge)	Performance Tasks
9	Understand the following: compare and contrast, terminology, self-evaluation, exemplars, analysis, and listening	1 Use a four-level rubric to evaluate a pre-recorded or live performance by self or others

Grade	Learning Target (Specific Knowledge)	Performance Tasks
10	Understand the following: compare and contrast, terminology, self-evaluation, exemplars, analysis, and listening	1 Use a four-level rubric to evaluate a pre-recorded or live performance by self or others

Grade	Learning Target (Specific Knowledge)		Performance Tasks
11	Understand the following: compare and contrast, terminology, self-evaluation, exemplars, analysis, and listening	1	Use a four-level rubric to evaluate a pre-recorded or live performance by self or others
12	Understand the following: compare and contrast, terminology, self-evaluation, exemplars, analysis, synthesis, and listening	1	Use a four-level rubric to evaluate a pre-recorded or live performance by self or others

7.E.2 Evaluate a given musical work in terms of its aesthetic qualities

Grade	Learning Target (Specific Knowledge)		Performance Tasks
9	Understand the music elements and terminology that apply to the aesthetic value of music (e.g., include how music affects our emotions or how aesthetic values vary from culture to culture)	1 2	Listen to and describe the aesthetic qualities of a musical performance Listen to two recordings of performances of the same work that differ sharply in interpretation and describe the aesthetic characteristics of each performance
10	Understand the music elements and terminology that apply to the aesthetic value of music (e.g., how music affects our emotions or how the aesthetic values vary from culture to culture)	1 2	Listen to and describe the aesthetic qualities of a musical performance Listen to two recordings of performances of the same work that differ sharply in interpretation and describe the aesthetic characteristics of each performance
11	Understand the music elements and terminology that apply to the aesthetic value of music (e.g., how music affects our emotions or how the aesthetic values vary from culture to culture)	1 2	Listen to and describe the aesthetic qualities of a musical performance Listen to two recordings of performances of the same work that differ sharply in interpretation and describe the aesthetic characteristics of each performance
12	Understand the music elements and terminology that apply to the aesthetic value of music (e.g., how music affects our emotions or how the aesthetic values vary from culture to culture)	1 2	Listen to and describe the aesthetic qualities of a musical performance Listen to two recordings of performances of the same work that differ sharply in interpretation and describe the aesthetic characteristics of each performance

Figure 39aa

8	MUSIC AND OTHER DISCIPLINES
	Students understand the relationship between music, the other arts, and other disciplines

8.8.1 Know how relationships expressed through music can be expressed differently through other art disciplines

Grade	Learning Target (Specific Knowledge)		Performance Tasks
5	Understand how events or emotions can be expressed in other arts disciplines (e.g., thunderstorm, sunrise, sorrow, surprise or excitement)	1	Identify how at least one event, scene, emotion, or concept in music might also be represented in one of the other arts (e.g., theater, dance and visual arts)
6	Understand how events or emotions can be expressed in other arts disciplines (e.g., thunderstorm, sunrise, sorrow, surprise or excitement)	1	Compare how various emotions, such as happiness, sadness, and excitement, are expressed in music, dance, theater, and visual arts and how they may be portrayed in each discipline
7	Understand how an event may be portrayed in other arts disciplines	1	Choose an event such as a social event or ceremony and give a description of how it might be portrayed in music, drama, visual art and dance
8	Make connections between music and math (rhythms are fractions), science (vibrations of sound), language arts (poetry), visual arts (lines similar to a piece of art), theater (musical theater), and dance (depicting emotions of music)	1	Create a presentation on how music is related to other subjects

8.8.2 Know how principles and concepts of other disciplines are related to those of music

Grade	Learning Target (Specific Knowledge)		Performance Tasks
5	Identify ways in which music is related to the surrounding world through school subjects and daily life	1	Identify at least one way that music is related to daily life or classes in science, math, history, or language arts
6	Identify ways in which music is related to the surrounding world through school subjects and daily life	1	Identify ways in which the world would change if music was not a part of it
7	Identify ways in which music is related to the surrounding world through school	1	Plan an integrated activity for another subject area to demonstrate how music ties in with other curriculum (e.g., music

Grade	Learning Target (Specific Knowledge)		Performance Tasks
8	Identify ways in which music is related to the surrounding world through school subjects and daily life	1	Study the effect of music and the ability to learn other subjects at a higher level than non-musicians in school
	Make connections between music and math (rhythms are fractions), science (vibrations of sound), language arts (poetry), visual arts (lines similar to a piece of art), theater (musical theater), and dance (depicting emotions of music)	2	Create a presentation on how music is related to other subjects

8.E.1   Know how artistic elements and processes are used in similar and distinctive ways in the various arts

Grade	Learning Target (Specific Knowledge)		Performance Tasks
9	Identify artistic elements and processes for selected art forms (e.g., unity, variety, texture, and craftsmanship)	1	Prepare a report or presentation identifying music in relationship to another art (e.g., visual art, dance, or drama); example: dancing to "Spring" from Vivaldi's *The Four Seasons* or drawing a picture to depict Rossini's *William Tell Overture*
10	Identify artistic elements and processes for selected art forms (e.g., unity, variety, texture, and craftsmanship)	1	Prepare a report on the state of two or more art forms during a particular time period
11	Identify artistic elements and processes for selected art forms (e.g., unity, variety, texture, and craftsmanship)	1	Prepare a report on the state of two or more art forms during a particular time period
12	Identify artistic elements and processes for selected art forms (e.g., unity, variety, texture, and craftsmanship) and demonstrate multimedia skills (e.g., audio, video, and computer skills)	1	Individually or with others prepare a multimedia presentation comparing and contrasting the arts areas within a specific historical period or a specific work of art (e.g., opera, ballet, or musical theater)

8.E.2 Understand the ways in which the principles and concepts of various disciplines outside the arts are related to those of music

Grade	Learning Target (Specific Knowledge)		Performance Tasks
9	Identify how the study of music is related to all current subjects	1	Prepare a brief report or presentation comparing skills involved in learning music and those used or learned in other subject areas; example: compare the ability of music and literature to convey images and emotions or describe the physical science of a string vibrating
10	Demonstrate how artistic elements are used in similar ways in various disciplines outside of the arts	1	Compare music to various non-arts forms to demonstrate how events, scenes, ideas, and emotions are represented in similar ways
10	Demonstrate how principles and concepts of various disciplines and life experiences outside of the arts are related to those of music	1	Identify examples in which the principles of non-arts disciplines and life experiences are related to those of music
11	Demonstrate how artistic elements are used in similar ways in various disciplines outside of the arts	1	Compare music to various non-arts forms to demonstrate how events, scenes, ideas, and emotions are represented in similar ways
11	Demonstrate how principles and concepts of various disciplines and life experiences outside of the arts are related to those of music	1	Identify examples in which the principles of non-arts disciplines and life experiences are related to those of music
12	Identify core principles of all subjects and use comparison and research skills	1	Prepare a brief report explaining how the principles and concepts of music are related to those of two disciplines outside the arts; examples: a compare the ability of music and literature to convey images, feelings, and meanings relevant to language arts b describe the physical basis of tone production in string, wind, percussion, electronic instruments, and the human voice, and describe the transmission and perception of sound relevant to physics

9   MUSIC, HISTORY AND CULTURE
Understand music in relation to history and culture

9.8.1   Know characteristics of music genres and styles from a variety of music cultures

Grade	Learning Target (Specific Knowledge)	Performance Tasks
5	Understand what characteristics are distinct in American folk songs, folk songs from other countries, and classical music	1 Perform music from various genres, styles, and cultures from a method book or literature; identify and describe the distinctive characteristics
6	Understand, identify, and describe music in various settings, cultures, and history	1 Discuss the setting of music for a symphony or rock concert, pow-wow, jam session, square dance, or performances in the Baroque and Classical eras
7	Understand, identify, and describe music in various settings, cultures, and history	1 Participate in a music listening contest, determining style, era, composer, and instrumentation of previously studied selections
8	Understand, identify, and describe music in various settings, cultures, and history	1 Compare and contrast two musical selections from two different cultures, countries, or eras of music

9.8.2 Know exemplary musical works from a variety of genres and styles

Grade	Learning Target (Specific Knowledge)	Performance Tasks
5	Know historical periods and events, composers, and titles	1 Listen to or perform selected music to learn about the composer and era
	Develop knowledge of orchestral classics	2 Listen to and perform famous works
6	Know historical periods and events, composers, and titles	1 Listen to or perform selected music to learn about the composer and era
	Develop knowledge of orchestral classics	2 Listen to and perform famous works
7	Know historical periods and events, composers, and titles	1 Listen to or perform selected music to learn about the composer and era
	Develop knowledge of orchestral classics	2 Listen to and perform famous works

Grade	Learning Target (Specific Knowledge)	Performance Tasks
8	Know historical periods and events, composers, and titles	1 Listen to or perform selected music to learn about the composer and era
	Develop knowledge of orchestral classics	2 Listen to and perform famous works

9.8.3 Know the functions of music, roles of musicians, and conditions of performance in several world cultures

Grade	Learning Target (Specific Knowledge)	Performance Tasks
55	Know and demonstrate proper audience behavior for the context and style of music performed in various cultural settings	1 Discuss the difference in behavior at school, rock, and symphony concerts

Grade	Learning Target (Specific Knowledge)	Performance Tasks
6	Know functions of music and the role of musicians for music performed in various cultural settings	1 Make comparisons of the function of music and the role of musicians at several different music events (e.g., pow-wow, Hindu religious service or African drumming event)

Grade	Learning Target (Specific Knowledge)	Performance Tasks
7	Know functions of music and the role of the musicians for music performed in various cultural settings	1 Research various musical roles in three different cultures (e.g., European opera singer, Japanese gamelan player, or Indian sitar player)

Grade	Learning Target (Specific Knowledge)	Performance Tasks
8	Understand various roles of musicians in musical occupations involving a sacred or secular ceremony, means of entertainment, or leisure from various cultures	1 Describe the role of a musician in three diverse cultures (e.g., the function served by the musician and the conditions under which they work; examples: a symphony orchestra conductor b church organist c composer of television commercials d middle-school choir director e rock band lead guitarist f talking drummer in sub-Saharan Africa g Indian sitar player h Peking opera singer I Japanese Kagaku court orchestra player j Japanese gamelan player

9.8.4 Demonstrate proper audience behavior

Grade	Learning Target (Specific Knowledge)	Performance Tasks
5	Know and demonstrate proper behavior for concert and classroom performance situations	1 Respect otherand audience members during a classroom or concert performance by being quiet and applauding at the appropriate times

Grade	Learning Target (Specific Knowledge)		Performance Tasks
6	Know and demonstrate proper behavior for concert and classroom performance situations	1	Respect otherand audience members during a classroom or concert performance by being quiet and applauding at the appropriate times

Grade	Learning Target (Specific Knowledge)		Performance Tasks
7	Know and demonstrate proper behavior for concert and classroom performance situations	1	Respect otherand audience members during a classroom or concert performance by being quiet and applauding at the appropriate times

Grade	Learning Target (Specific Knowledge)		Performance Tasks
8	Know and demonstrate proper behavior for concert and classroom performance situations	1	Respect otherand audience members during a classroom or concert performance by being quiet and applauding at the appropriate times

9.E.1 Know the representative examples of music from a variety of cultures and historical periods

Grade	Learning Target (Specific Knowledge)		Performance Tasks
9	Identify elements, composers, and musical examples of basic Western music history (e.g., Baroque, Classical, Romantic, Impressionistic, and 20th Century)	1	Complete assignments in the process of learning and listening to examples regarding music history
9	Identify elements of music from a variety of cultures	1	Listen to music from America, Africa, Asia, or other cultures and describe the elements of each When given unfamiliar listening examples,identify which culture is represented in the music performed
10	Identify elements, composers, and musical examples of basic Western music history (e.g., Baroque, Classical, Romantic, Impressionistic, and 20th Century)	1	Prepare a report about a composition describing its genre, style, historical period, composer, and its historical and cultural context
10	Identify elements of music from a variety of cultures	1	Listen to music from America, Africa, Asia, or other cultures and describe the elements of each When given unfamiliar listening examples,identify which culture is represented in the music performed
11	Identify elements, composers, and musical examples of basic Western music history (e.g., Baroque, Classical, Romantic, Impressionistic, and 20th Century)	1	Prepare a report about a composition describing its genre, style, historical period, composer, and its historical and cultural context

Grade	Learning Target (Specific Knowledge)		Performance Tasks
11	Identify elements of music from a variety of cultures	1	Listen to music from America, Africa, Asia, or other cultures and describe the elements of each When given unfamiliar listening examples,identify which culture is represented in the music performed

Grade	Learning Target (Specific Knowledge)		Performance Tasks
12	Know genre, style, historical period or culture, composers and performers, historical and cultural contexts	1	Study several pieces representing a style or culture, listen to unfamiliar pieces selected by teacher and describe how the piece is or is not representative of the particular style

9.E.2 Know sources of American music, the evolution of these genres and musicians associated with them

Grade	Learning Target (Specific Knowledge)		Performance Tasks
9	Identify forms of American music (e.g., swing, Broadway musical, folk, jazz, and blues)	1	Listen to various forms of music, learn composers and performers of this style, and play examples of these styles
10	Know the history and styles of jazz (e.g., performers, composers, and characteristics)	1	Listen to various styles of jazz and learn about the composers of each style and, if possible, play examples
11	Know history, styles, and examples of Broadway musicals	1	Listen to examples of Broadway musicals, learn about the composers, and, if possible, play examples
12	Know history, styles, and examples of contemporary/popular music (e.g., rock and country)	1	Listen to examples of contemporary/popular music and learn about the composers/performers and, if possible, play examples

9.E.3 Know the various roles that musicians perform and representative individuals who have functioned in each role

Grade	Learning Target (Specific Knowledge)		Performance Tasks
9	Identify job descriptions of musical careers (e.g., entertainer, teacher, sound technician, music therapist, music store manager, music editor, or publisher	1	Write a brief description of a musical profession in which they may want to be involved including the education needed and duties of the position
10	Study music careers/roles in history (e.g., composers, performers, entertainers, teachers, managers, music editor/publisher, sound technician, and music therapists)	1	Research and give a presentation on a career or musical role

Grade	Learning Target (Specific Knowledge)		Performance Tasks
11	Study music careers/roles in history (e.g., composers, performers, entertainers, teachers, managers, music editor/publisher, sound technician, and music therapists)	1	Research and give a presentation on a career or musical role

Grade	Learning Target (Specific Knowledge)		Performance Tasks
12	Study music careers/roles in history (e.g., composers, performers, entertainers, teachers, managers, music editor/publisher, sound technician, and music therapists)	1	Interview a community member asking about the person's musical background, training, involvement, and the role of music within that person's life
		2	Research and give a presentation on a career or musical role

10 Understand how to take care of and tune instrument

10.8.1 Understand how to take care of and tune instrument

Grade	Learning Target (Specific Knowledge)		Performance Tasks
5	Know the parts of the instrument and bow and understand how to pack and unpack the instrument, rosin the bow, tighten and loosen the bow, clean off rosin when putting it away, and how to prevent accidents	1	Study a chart of the parts of the instrument and bow and practice packing and unpacking the instrument, tightening, loosening, and rosining the bow on a daily basis Theshould also know about weather changes and how they affect their instruments
6	Demonstrate proper care of the instrument and bow along with choice of quality strings and checking tuner depth underneath the fine tuners	1	Learn about the quality of strings and how to check fine tuners during a brief "instrument care clinic" held at the beginning of the year or periodically throughout the yearunderstand when repairs are needed and who makes the repairs
7	Demonstrate proper care and maintenance of the instrument and bow, including frequency of string changes and bow re-hairing	1	Learn about the quality of strings and how to check fine tuners during a brief "instrument care clinic" held at the beginning of the year or periodically throughout the yearunderstand when repairs are needed and who makes the repairs
8	Understand the value of a step-up instrument and what to look for when purchasing one	1	Study the characteristics of a quality instrument and how to take care of it

10.8.2	Tune instrument

Grade	Learning Target (Specific Knowledge)		Performance Tasks
5	Know when a string is out of tune	1	Can determine if a string is out of tune and, in some cases, tune with the assistance of teacher
6	Identify if a string is in or out of tune to an audible pitch and properly tune using only the fine tuners with teacher's guidance	1	Match the tuning note by adjusting the pitch using fine tuners on a daily basis with the assistance of teacher
7	Demonstrate how to properly use fine tuners when matching an audible pitch with minimal instructor guidance	1	Match the tuning note and adjust the pitch using fine tuners on a daily basis with minimal teacher guidance
8	Demonstrate how to tune the instrument properly using fine tuners and pegs when matching an audible pitch with minimal instructor guidance	1	Match the tuning note and adjust the pitch using fine tuners and pegs with minimal instructor guidance

10.E.2	Demonstrate proper care of the instrument and bow

Grade	Learning Target (Specific Knowledge)		Performance Tasks
9	Understand the value of a step-up instrument and what to look for when purchasing one	1	Study the characteristics of a quality instrument and how to take care of it
10	Understand the value of a step-up instrument and what to look for when purchasing one	1	Study the characteristics of a quality instrument and how to take care of it
11	Understand the value of a step-up instrument and what to look for when purchasing one	1	Study the characteristics of a quality instrument and how to take care of it
12	Understand the value of a step-up instrument and what to look for when purchasing one	1	Study the characteristics of a quality instrument and how to take care of it

10.E.2 Tune instrument independently

Grade	Learning Target (Specific Knowledge)	Performance Tasks
9	Demonstrate how to tune the instrument properly using fine tuners and pegs when matching an audible pitch independently	1 Match the tuning note and adjust the pitches of each string using fine tuners and pegs with no teacher assistance
10	Demonstrate how to tune the instrument properly using fine tuners and pegs when matching an audible pitch independently	1 Match the tuning note and adjust the pitches of each string using fine tuners and pegs with no teacher assistance
11	Demonstrate how to tune the instrument properly using fine tuners and pegs when matching an audible pitch independently	1 Match the tuning note and adjust the pitches of each string using fine tuners and pegs with no teacher assistance
12	Demonstrate how to tune the instrument properly using fine tuners and pegs when matching an audible pitch independently	1 Match the tuning note and adjust the pitches of each string using fine tuners and pegs with no teacher assistance

Resources and Websites

RESOURCES

Bloom, B. (1956). *Taxonomy of Educational Objectives.* New York: David McKay Chappuis, J. and Chappuis, S. (2002). *Understanding School Assessment: A Parent and Community Guide to helping Students Learn.* Portland, OR: Assessment Training Institute.

Chappuis S., Stiggins, R., Arter J., & Chappuis, J. (2005). *Assessment for Learning: An Action Guide for School Leaders.* Portland, OR: Assessment Training Institute.

Easton, L. (2004). *Powerful Designs for Professional Learning.* Oxford, OH: National Staff Development Council.

Marzano, R., Pickering, D., & Pollock, J. (2001). *Classroom Instruction That Works: Research-Based Strategies for Increasing Student Achievement.* Alexandria, VA: Association for Supervision and Curriculum Development.

Marzano, R. (2006). *Designing a New Taxonomy of Educational Objectives.* Thousand Oaks, CA: Corwin Books.

MENC. (1994) *National Standards for Arts Education: What Every Young American Should Know and Be Able to do in the Arts.* Virginia: MENC.

MENC. (1996) *Performance Standards for Music.* Virginia: MENC.

Stiggins, R., Arter, J., Chappuis, J., & Chappuis, S. (2004). *Classroom Assessment for Student Learning: Doing it Right-Using it Well.* Portland, OR: Assessment Training Institute.

Wormeli, R. (2006). *Fair Isn't Always Equal.* Portland, MA: Stenhouse Publishers.

Wiggins, G. & McTighe, J. (2005). *Understanding by Design*, 2nd Edition. Alexandria, VA: Association for Supervision and Curriculum Development.

WEBSITES

Association for Supervision and Curriculum Development	http://www.ascd.org
Fargo Public Schools Music Content Standards	http://fmpro1.fargo.k12.nd.us/standards/
Mid-continent Research for Education and Learning	http://mcrel.org
National Association for Music Education	http://menc.org/

About the Author

Denese Odegaard has taught fifth-through-ninth-grade orchestra for twenty-eight years and is currently the Fargo Public Schools Drama and Music Curriculum Specialist.

On a national level, she contributed to the MENC (National Association for Music Education) publication *Standards and Benchmarks for Composition and Arranging.* She is currently President-elect of the North Central Division of MENC and past Secretary for ASTA (American String Teacher Association).

On a state level, she served on the writing committee for the North Dakota Fine Arts Standards. She has been president of the North Dakota String Teachers Association and the North Dakota Music Educators Association.

At the district level, Odegaard is a member of the District Assessment Committee, Activities Council, Curriculum Council, and chairs the Performing Arts Committee.

She has presented sessions on curriculum and assessment at the Midwest Clinic, ASTA Conferences, MENC conferences, and state conferences in Texas, Ohio, Illinois, Indiana, Iowa, and North Dakota, and at Integrating Curriculum, Theory, and Practice: A Symposium on Assessment in Music Education in 2007 and 2009.

Odegaard has contributed to *Teaching Music Through Performance in Orchestra, Volume Three* (GIA) and *Assessment in Music Education: Integrating Curriculum, Theory, and Practice: Proceedings of the 2007 Symposium on Assessment in Music Education* (GIA). She has also been invited to contribute to *Best Teaching Practices for Reaching all Learners: What Award-Winning Classroom Teachers Do* (Corwin Press).

She was named North Dakota String Teacher of the Year in 2005. In 2006, she received the Lois Bailey Glenn Award for Teaching Excellence from The National Music Foundation and has been presented the ASTA Citation for Leadership and Merit in 2006 and 2008.